Advance Praise for *The Politics of Lonely*

"A friend-letter (which is like a love-letter, but more complicated) to the ordinary glory of being with others, in all our mess and beauty, *The Politics of Lonely* is an incisive call to build worlds in which friendship is more and more accessible, for everyone."

—**ALEXIS SHOTWELL**, author of *Against Purity: Living Ethically in Compromised Times*

"There are few things as mundane in our lives as friendship, but also, few things as important that are also as unprobed. What makes a friend? What do we need from others? How do our relationships buoy our happiness or exacerbate our loneliness? Lee Arden has given us a lot to think about in this radical examination of one of society's most important social bonds."

—**NORA LORETO**, author of *The Social Safety Net*

"*The Politics of Lonely* made me feel less lonely. Yes, this is a book that invokes the radical potential of queer friendship—all the dreams and aspirations—without neglecting to address the personal, intimate, and structural failures. Drawing from a wide variety of voices in literature, critical thinking—and, yes, friendship—this book moves us toward everyday intimacy, collaboration, mutual aid, protest, communal living, and an expansion of care networks to provide a safety net for everyone."

—**MATTILDA BERNSTEIN SYCAMORE**, author of *Terry Dactyl*

"Lee Arden offers a thoughtful meditation on what austerity has done to our friendships, with a pragmatic and radically grounded pathway to transform and rebuild a social safety net in the spaces between us."

—**ARDATH WHYNACHT**, author of *Insurgent Love*

"Arden's exploration of friendship as 'the highest ideal of love' is essential medicine for these dehumanizing times. It is neither bitter pill nor sugarcoated remedy for what ails our ability to make friendship live up to our aspirations. Instead, it is dreamily homeopathic, mixing up a tonic to strengthen our broken hearts. It is at once vulnerable and brave, messily honest and truly beautiful, deeply personal and systemically political, reminding us that friendship is 'worth the struggle,' as part and parcel of social transformation."

—**CINDY BARUKH MILSTEIN**, editor of *Constellations of Care: Anarcha-Feminism in Practice*

THE POLITICS OF LONELY

WHY IS FRIENDSHIP SO HARD?

LEE ARDEN

Fernwood Publishing
Halifax and Winnipeg

Development editing: Fazeela Jiwa
Copyediting: Brenda Conroy
Cover design: Rebecca Poulin
Text design: Lauren Jeanneau
Printed and bound in the UK

Published by Fernwood Publishing
Halifax and Winnipeg
2970 Oxford Street, Halifax, Nova Scotia, B3L 2W4
fernwoodpublishing.ca

Fernwood Publishing Company Limited gratefully acknowledges the financial support of the Government of Canada through the Canada Book Fund and the Canada Council for the Arts..

Canada | Canada Council for the Arts | Conseil des arts du Canada

Library and Archives Canada Cataloguing in Publication
Title: The politics of lonely : why is friendship so hard? / Lee Arden.
Names: Arden, Lee, author.
Description: Includes bibliographical references and index.
Identifiers: Canadiana 20260169463 | ISBN 9781773638263 (softcover)
Subjects: LCSH: Friendship. | LCSH: Friendship—Sociological aspects. | LCSH: Loneliness—Social aspects. | LCSH: Interpersonal relations.
Classification: LCC BF575.F66 A73 2026 | DDC 302.34—dc23

Contents

Marsha panhandled for spare change, and she would say, "Spare change for a starving queen?" Most of that money, she didn't keep. She gave it to other girls who were struggling. If you were walking down the street, and she saw that you were hungry, and she had two slices of pizza, she might not give you one slice, she might give you both of them.

—RENEE IMPERATO, remembering Marsha P. Johnson

This book is dedicated to everyone who aspires to be this good a friend but hasn't made it there yet.

PREFACE

Friendship Is Worth the Struggle

I wrote this book not because I think I'm great at friendship but because it matters a lot to me. I think about it so much, and I still profoundly struggle to be the kind of friend I want to be and to have the kinds of friendships I want to have. I am far from alone in this. Articles with titles like "The Scheduling Woes of Adult Friendship," "How to Make, and Keep, Friends in Adulthood," and "Why Does Growing Up and Settling Down Mean Losing a Certain Closeness with Your Friends?" point to widespread struggles with making and maintaining friendships.[1] There's even a *Making Friends as an Adult for Dummies* book. It's hard to make or have friends after thirty, people agree, or once you have kids. But why? It's a common issue but surely there's nothing inherent to adulthood that means you can't have friends anymore.

The first thing I wrote about friendship was a zine called *PALS: The Radical Possibilities of Friendship*, which I put out in 2013. I was about to leave my last straight relationship, quit a terrible job, and transition. I was about to lose a lot and gain the entire shape of my life to come. But it wasn't there yet, and I had no idea it was coming. I just knew that my current life was completely untenable and that I was right at the end of my ability to continue living it. I wasn't eating or sleeping much, and I was having panic attacks every day, mean and scared and shaking and miserable. I was looking at checking myself in someplace, but I am glad something inside me knew that what I needed was to quit something, and then quit something else, and keep quitting things until the pressure started to release.

In that moment the only thing I felt sure of was friendship. I was struggling in my romantic, familial, and professional relationships, but in my friendships I still felt borne up. My friends were the only people I felt able to be around while I was in freefall, with everything in my life crumbling underneath me and no idea where I was going to land. My friends showed me care and kindness, and our relationships were spacious enough that I did not feel like I was failing them by being messy and sad and unsure of everything.

As I emerged from that period of my life into queer and trans communities, it seemed like everyone around me also held friendship up as their priority and the highest ideal of love. We spoke of chosen families where we would be loved just as we were, unlike the rejections many of us experienced in our families of origin. We daydreamed together about expansive friendships that could transcend the scripts we'd grown up with that centred romantic love and the nuclear family. It didn't need to be like that! We could remake everything in our own queer image. In this spirit, I wrote in ***PALS*** about some aspects of friendship that I thought differentiated it in important ways from other types of relationships:

- Friendship is, or can be, a meeting among equals.
- Friendship has more flexibility built into it, because our ideas of what a friendship can look like are less determinate and more varied than our ideas about relationships like parenthood or monogamous romance.
- Investing in friendship and taking it as the model for how we relate to other people can point us toward a practice of mutual aid, where we expand our sense of who we must care for and who we may accept care from, beyond the couple or nuclear family.
- Friendship, similar to and in combination with romantic nonmonogamy, can orient us away from thinking of our relationships in terms of scarcity.

In many ways the book you're reading now intends to both build on and question these ideas about friendship based on the experiences I've had in the years since writing the zine. Because of ***PALS***, I've had so many conversations with my own friends and with strangers and new acquaintances about what friendship means to them. I have heard about so many people's meaningful friendships and have been given opportunities to reflect on and appreciate my own. These conversations have strengthened my belief that friendship is a vital fount of joy and meaning in life, and that it can be a bridge that leads us out of ourselves and into solidarity and engagement with the broader world. Friendship often gets treated as an extracurricular activity: something to be scheduled in amongst all your other obligations, time permitting. But I've come to see it as the very fabric of life itself.

When Friendship Breaks Your Heart

In spite of, or because of, all the faith and hope and effort I have put into friendship, it has often broken my heart. My experiences of friendship and my views on it have become more complicated and less rosy than they were in 2013, when I wrote *PALS*. In particular, getting top surgery in 2017 was a turning point in my relationship with friendship. The lead-up to that surgery — a few years after putting out *PALS*, a few years into immersion in queer and trans communities — was the high-water mark for my optimism about friendship. My relationship with friendship has been more complex and more guarded since then.

A few years before that, my boyfriend at the time had top surgery. The majority of his care fell to me, I cracked under it, and we broke up soon after. So, when I was planning my own top surgery, I was determined that my then-girlfriend wouldn't have to provide an amount of care that would overtax her or our relationship. I talked to a lot of friends about it and made note of anyone who offered to help. I diligently made a little spreadsheet of what I'd need and when and invited people to sign up for anything they wanted to help with. Community! Chosen family! I was confident that I had it covered. And then almost everyone bailed. So, in the aftermath of my surgery, it was my girlfriend who kept me fed, took me to appointments, ran errands, and soothed me when I was scared and weak and in pain.

I am fortunate to have many close friends, but they're scattered across the continent and the world. Most of them are busy. Most of them are dealing with so much of their own shit that I'm scared to ask them for help. I'm not sure if it'd be OK to ask them to bring me food, wash my dishes, lift things down from high shelves. And of course, it wasn't that I was a perfect friend who was tragically let down by others. I can't live up to my own lofty ideals either, although I know the point of ideals isn't to consistently, flawlessly meet them — it's to strive messily and continuously toward them and to keep trying and failing and trying. I am as likely as anyone to be selfish or careless or cruel, and when I let someone down or cut them loose or otherwise fail to live up to my own values and aspirations, I feel extra shame for having presumed to lecture people about friendship. I've felt shame when I've failed to live up to my own ideas of how a friendship should be or to a friend's desires about the role they'd like me to play in their life. I've felt shame when, despite putting so much thought and care and work into building and maintaining friendships, I find I can't rely on my friends in ways I'd hoped I could. And I've felt shame when friendship can't take the place of romantic or familial care in the ways I dreamed of. In these moments I hold my optimistic little zine up against a sometimes disappointing reality, and I wonder why I fall short. Friendship is something I've devoted so much time and energy and thought to, and when it doesn't do what I hope it will, I feel curiosity as well as sadness.

I wondered if it was something about me and the way I do friendship or whether there were larger social factors keeping my friendships from rising to the level of my hopes and intentions. I became curious about how other people organize their lives and relationships, and about how we can work within and around the constraints of a capitalist society even as we also work to dismantle it and build something better.

Friendship Is Hard Because Everything Is Hard

People are lonely and struggling in friendships because of the historical, cultural, economic, and material ways that our lives are set up. These factors are not timeless and inevitable: things can be otherwise. There are people benefiting from our loneliness and seeking to perpetuate it for their own gain. It would really cut into AI chatbots' profit margins if we all had people to talk to; meal delivery apps would suffer if we cooked for each other more; and Mark Zuckerberg and Elon Musk would hate it if we went for a walk with a friend instead of doomscrolling.

Material conditions matter a lot, regardless of our ideals. In Canada, where I live, as well as in many other parts of the world, our social safety net is profoundly degraded, and the cost of housing and other necessities of life have exploded while wages have remained stagnant. My friends are in and out of homelessness, or they're disabled and fighting to get or hold on to meagre state benefits, or they're trans and trying to get healthcare, or they're facing violent racism, or they're scared for family members abroad who are facing genocide or climate crisis or immigration detention, or they're fighting alt-right weirdos in the street, or they are struggling with any combination of the above. Things are rough out there.

Is it any surprise that this affects our ability to show up and care for each other? When my friends are kicked out of their families of origin, have lost access to their cultural ties through colonization and forced migration, or grew up in situations of abuse, violence, religious trauma, neglect, poverty, and so on, it would be nice if friendship could take the place of everything they've lost, but it's a lot to ask. Friendship alone can't pick up the slack from decades of austerity, unravelled social safety nets, or the crushing combination of bullshit wages and exorbitant rents.

We will try, and we will fail, to make the power of our love for our friends as big and as strong as the destructive power of the state. The answer isn't to stop trying or to be more moderate in our ambitions. We need to keep trying in our personal lives to live up to the ideals we hold dear. We also need to keep fighting for massive changes to the way we live, to break down systems of violence, and to build systems of care. In the meantime, I have found that placing friendship in a broader political context has helped me understand why our friendships work the way they do. When you're barely getting by, it can be a lot harder to show up for your friends. If you have slack, you can share the slack around. If you aren't strapped for cash, you can help friends out when they're stuck. If every room and closet and semi-enclosed nook in your apartment isn't stuffed full of roommates to share the rent, you can host out-of-town pals to keep those friendships strong or put a friend up when they lose their home. If time is abundant, it's easier to babysit or help someone move or just keep each other company.

It is beautiful to have expansive hopes and dreams for our friendships, but when we fail to look at them in context and see all the external pressures placed on them, we'll end up hurting and disappointing each other. We know that people will always share what little they have. Every marginalized community seems to make that joke about everyone just passing around the same $20 to whomever needs it most at the moment. And we know that the people with least are often the most generous. But the solution is not to squeeze everyone just to the edge of their breaking point so they'll be more giving. I believe the solution is, first, to become aware of the ways austerity and other forms of structural violence show up in our close relationships and to cut ourselves some slack. Then, clearer-eyed, we can start tearing down the institutions that keep us separate, lonely, and struggling. Throughout this book we'll look at ways that friendship can act as a gateway drug for community and for political action: how it can both fill our hearts and serve as a powerful force for building a better world.

There's a great Lucinda Williams song where she sings in an intimidating growl to presumably some shitty ex, "You took my joy, I want it back." She repeats it over and over like she's driving through the night coming to take back her joy by any means necessary. This is the energy I want us all to bring forward with our friendships. Let's find the fuckers (spoiler: capitalism, neoliberalism, austerity, white supremacy, jobs) who took our joy and get it back.

Despite It All, We Come Through for Each Other

I started writing this book in 2023, six years after my top-surgery friendship failure, while I was preparing for another surgery. I was reflecting a lot on my previous experience, both in pragmatic ways to think about what I would need to do differently and also against my will because I was just deeply triggered about it. I was having nightmares about helplessness and abandonment. My fear was that I would tumble through another false floor and have another realization that a baseline of care that I had thought I could rely on was not there.

This time everything went really well. I don't know if it's just that I was older and my friends were also older: more aware of our responsibilities to each other, more experienced in providing care, in some cases more resourced, and with more experience with sickness and disability. The care I received buoyed me up as I began to write this book and gave me enough optimism and curiosity to keep looking at friendship rather than simply writing it off. If and when I do friendship and care well it is because I have been lucky beyond reason or measure in the friendship and care I've been shown. In spite of how difficult friendship is in our current world, it is a source of both tremendous joy and vital material support in my life.

In tribute to my friends and to the many wise people I interviewed about friendship while writing this book, I have woven their voices into the book. Between the chapters, which detail my experiences and beliefs around friendship, you'll also find interludes with several different people's answers to questions I posed about friendship. My hope is that you will take these interludes as an opportunity to pause and reflect on your own answers.

WHAT ARE SOME WAYS YOU'VE CARED FOR YOUR FRIENDS?

I have driven people to appointments and vacations when they're unable to do so. I like driving and I don't mind doing a lot of it, so I tend to offer it as an act of service. I show tenderness in my words and in my touch. I affirm and reaffirm my love for people. I offer my perspective when it's desired and help problem solve or else provide space/an open ear. I'm proud of my keen attention to others' needs and my willingness to support people.

—MARLAINA

Small acts, constantly! I try and make sure that my friends know I think about them, remember and value things they have told me or their preferences that I've noticed. Bringing little gifts that reminded me of them, unprompted, or sharing things that connect to their interests in some way. I aspire to have my friends be sure that I care for them, and I think this is the case already. I personally have some issues with accepting that my friends think of me as highly as I do of them, so I perhaps say reassurances more often and knowingly, since that is what I want in response as well.

—ERIN

I think, underneath everything I do, I just want to be someone safe. I was a lonely kid and felt like nobody really wanted me around; worse than that I felt like nobody wanted to learn enough about me to have a ***reason*** not to want me around. I don't want other people to experience that, ever. So, I just do my best to notice. I pay attention to my friends. I think, if I was this person, what would be meaningful to me? What would make my life noticeably better? And then I try to make it happen, whatever it is.

—CARA

PART ONE

WHAT IS FRIENDSHIP?

Friendship is a pretty ambiguous concept. While that ambiguity can be both beautiful and useful, it can also contribute to our struggles to get what we need and want from our friendships. Throughout Part 1 of this book, I look at what friendship even is, examining my own received conceptions of friendship to see how they hold up in real life.

In Chapter 1, "Do We Even Know What Friendship Is?," I write about how, in the white, middle-class, North American social world I grew up in, I've experienced friendship as a relationship that is nebulous and flexible: it is more easily defined by what it isn't (romance, family) than what it is, and it is often held to less clear and demanding standards than those other categories of relationship. How does this flexibility benefit our friendships, and how would we be better off if our friends held us to more rigorous standards?

Chapter 2, "Casual Sex, Serious Friendships, and Life Outside the Couple," describes how, in a heteronormative world, although friendship encompasses a broad range of relationships, we still believe it can and should be firmly distinguished from romance and treated as secondary to romantic and familial relationships. What happens in the grey areas where friendship, love, sex, and commitment are combined in less normative ways?

Chapter 3, "Weaving Networks of Friendship," begins by looking at dictionary definitions that characterize friendship as a non-exclusive relationship between two people; that is, we're allowed to have lots of friends. I examine what happens when we take this non-exclusivity further and weave our friendships together instead of treating them as distinct one-on-one relationships.

In Chapter 4, "The Families We Choose," I look at the concept of "chosen family," an idea that shapes the concepts of friendships I see in the queer and trans spaces I am in. We tend to hope that chosen families can be a way to avoid all the bad or hard things we've experienced in our families of origin. Where did the concept of friends as chosen family come from, and what can we learn from its origins?

Let's prod at these ideas of friendship, look at where they come from, and think about which ones we'd rather do differently.

ONE

Do We Even Know What Friendship Is?

> One to joke with and one to confide problems in; one to live with and one to romance with; one to go to the cinema with and others to dine with.
>
> —HENNING BECH, describing different types of friends in *When Men Meet: Homosexuality and Modernity*[1]

Friendship often feels to me like it's made up of leftovers that don't fall under other, more clearly defined types of relationships. Although romantic relationships can look many kinds of ways, we tend to be able to recognize those when we see them. There are also many configurations of family relationships, but when they are solidified by blood or legal bonds, we understand where to put them. Is friendship just defined by what it isn't? Is a friend just someone you care about but are not having sex with, related to, or spending time with primarily for financial reasons, like a coworker? You probably have a pretty nebulous idea of what friendship looks like compared to what marriage looks like. You might refer to any of the following people as friends:

- someone you have known for decades, who you'd trust with your life, who you wouldn't hesitate to ask to feed your cat if you were out of town
- someone you regularly do an activity with but don't really interact with outside of that context or have conversations with other than about your shared activity
- someone you drink or party with
- someone you work with and don't hate
- someone you see around, and know people in common with, and occasionally talk to
- someone you went to high school with and catch up with every couple years
- someone you text back and forth with every once and a while and see around
- a mutual on social media.

There are people I consider a friend who wouldn't consider me theirs, and vice versa. There are people I consider close friends who do not think of me the same way, and vice versa. My dreams and goals for the friendship probably differ from those of my friends. Friendship is flexible in that it's a category that contains an array of relationships that are substantially different from one other. This also grants friendships flexibility over time because they can change so deeply while remaining in the category of "friendship" without prompting a conversation about whether the relationship is still working out for everyone involved or whether it even still constitutes a friendship. This comes in part from the fact that the state is not involved in friendship in the way it is in romantic and family relationships. There is no legal status of friend, no way of solemnizing and formalizing a friendship in the eyes of the law, like marriage or adoption formalizes a romantic or familial relationship. But our friendships might be well served by having more conversations about them and maybe by making them more formal, even if I'd rather the state not get involved.

In the white North American context I grew up in, we are not encouraged to be very intentional about friendship — to ask "what are we to each other?" or "where do you see this going?" or "how would you like things to be between us?" in the way that is expected and encouraged in a romantic relationship. In her book *Ace: What Asexuality Reveals about Desire, Society, and the Meaning of Sex*, Angela Chen writes, "Many people are hesitant to say "I love you" to friends, much less ask, "How do you feel about time? What are we to each other?"[2] As one of her interviewees noted, "Outside of romance, there is no 'defining the relationship' talk unless something has already gone wrong." I would also add this question: "How do we want to present our relationship to other people in our life and ask to be understood and treated by them?" Because your close friendships — your friendships that butt up against the borders placed between different types of relationships — will be scrutinized and questioned. If you spend too much time together, share too much of your life, commit to and prioritize one another, people will, for better or for worse, want to know where to situate you in relationship to one another. I talk more about this — the relationship between friendship and romance — in the next chapter.

Different Friendships in Different Contexts

Sometimes I've rejoiced in how the category of "friendship" can contain so many different types of relationships. But the ambiguity of friendship and its lack of common scripts can also cause trouble. In romantic relationships there is more cultural knowledge to draw on, even though a lot of it is misogynistic and focused on straight, monogamous relationships between cis people. It's still a body of knowledge you can draw on, adapt, or explicitly reject when you're navigating romantic relationships. But I have found fewer stories and archetypes about friendship to guide me through difficulty. Because friendships are often seen as expendable in a way that romantic relationships aren't, I have had fewer models for how to be a good friend, how to work on my friendships, and how to deal with conflict, abuse, hurt, disappointment, and mismatched expectations.

I write from my own context as a white person of English and Irish heritage who has lived my whole life in North America. Other cultural contexts may define friendship more narrowly. For example, in the article "What Are Friends for in Russia Versus Canada?: An Approach for Documenting Cross-Cultural Differences,"[3] the authors quote from *Lost in Translation*, the 1989 memoir of Eva Hoffman, who was born in Poland shortly after World War II and moved to North America in her early teens. She writes of someone in her life:

> We like each other quite well, though I'm not sure what is between us is "friendship" — a word which in Polish has connotations of strong loyalty and

> attachment bordering on love. At first, I try to preserve the distinction between "friends" and "acquaintances" scrupulously, because it feels like a small lie to say "friend" when you don't really mean it, but after a while I give it up. "Friend," in English, is such a good-natured, easygoing sort of term, covering all kinds of territory, and "acquaintance" is something an uptight, snobbish person might say … As the word is used here, [she] is certainly a friend.

This demonstrates a cultural difference in what friends can expect from each other. The article's authors also cite an older article comparing Ghanaian and North American concepts of friendships, finding that "Ghanaian participants advocated caution toward friends and emphasized practical assistance as a defining characteristic of friendship. They also saw having many friends as foolish, because of the heavy obligations that come with friendship."[4] The authors identified both Ghanaian and Russian concepts of friendship as more demanding than the Anglo-American one: friendship was not a relationship you entered into lightly, because once you are friends with someone, you have a strong obligation toward them. This observation was corroborated by my friend Veronika, who described growing up in Germany with a Russian conception of friendship:

> Now that I'm an adult I realize how important my mother's friends were in raising me and my siblings … Most of my mother's friends moved from the same village in Siberia thirty plus years ago to Germany

> and they all asked to be placed into housing in a similar region, so that they would be close to each other. They still live near each other and regularly visit, and celebrate their birthdays, the new year, and other events together. So, it's this group of around six women who have known each other since childhood, and are still close … And they helped to raise each other's children! As a child I spent a lot of time with my "aunts" and "uncles" (in Russia every older person who is friends with your parents is called aunt or uncle) because my parents both worked double jobs with long working hours. I spent a similar amount of time in the care of my "aunts" as with my mother. For a long time I didn't even understand the distinction of who is my "real aunt" and who isn't. They all divided their time of caretaking, wage-paying jobs and building houses between each other (even the friends who didn't have children) ... In retrospect it's incredible to see how they all connected and stayed in touch. Especially because most of them have difficult/abusive relationships with their husbands, and I have heard them supporting each other in their struggles.

Though these are just a few examples, they show very different conceptions of friendship than the less defined and often less involved North American one. I don't mean to simplify the broad diversity of ways that interpersonal relationships have been organized across place and time. But learning that there were conceptions of friendship that were more robust and demanding than the ones I grew up with made me both reflect on the ways that friendship is shaped by cultural context and grieve that the ones I grew up with seemed flimsy and wishy-washy. In many ways I appreciate the flexibility of friendship in white North America — that our friendships are given more space to change and fluctuate over time. Our other relationships, especially romantic relationships, could probably use more of this type of flexibility and openness to change. These other relationships often have impossibly narrow and detailed standards to live up to in a way that friendships don't.

Like many people with cultural backgrounds similar to my own, I don't consider friendship as constituting a promise in the way that I would be inclined to consider a romantic or familial relationship as a promise. When I enter a romantic relationship with someone, I generally understand that the relationship will continue to be a romantic one until someone decides otherwise. And if anyone in the relationship wants to change the form the relationship takes, there will be a conversation about it. This isn't generally the case for the friendships I've experienced. It's been interesting for me to learn that a sense of casualness in entering and exiting friendships and a belief that friendship does not constitute an especially strong obligation is culturally specific, not universal.

In my own experience there isn't necessarily a strong obligation to be there for a friend who is in need. There isn't a strong social cost to bailing. If a friend asks too much of you, whatever that looks like, people will tell you that you are within your rights to cut them off, that you don't owe them anything. This is something I've talked about a lot with one of my friends, who's expressed skepticism and fear about whether bonds of friendship in queer communities can really fulfill the role that a family of origin does for people who have close and loving ties with their family of origin, or that a committed relationship does for people who are in those. If you were in prison would your friends visit you, not once or twice but every week? Would your friends take you in if you couldn't live on your own?

I was raised WASP (white Anglo-Saxon Protestant), a culture that takes whiteness' individualism and abhorrence of vulnerability to its limits. Acknowledging my interdependence with others does not come easily to me; I feel more at home trying to do everything myself, and bottling up any inconvenient feelings I may have about it. So, when I think of the flexibility of friendships, I can admit that sometimes the option to fade away and leave can be more appealing to me than the option to come closer, drop by uninvited, or respond to greater needs with greater closeness and care.

Over the decade or so that friendship has preoccupied me as one of the primary themes I think and write about, I have made a conscious effort to invest more deeply in my friendships: allow them to take up more space and time in my life, and provide and accept a greater depth and breadth of care. However, doing this has also caused me to crash, over and over, into the invisible but strictly enforced boundaries between friendship and romance.

TWO

Casual Sex, Serious Friendships, and Life Outside the Couple

> At [the leather bar] the Catacombs, even brief connections were handled with courtesy and care. And there was a particular kind of love that emerged from the [fisting] slings. Sometimes that love only happened in "the back." Just as often, it extended out into the everyday world. The Catacombs facilitated the formation of important friendships and lasting networks of support. Many of the men who frequented the Catacombs found relationships there that have sustained them through time, nurtured them with affection, cared for them in sickness, and buried them in sorrow.
>
> —GAYLE RUBIN, "The Catacombs: A Temple of the Butthole"[1]

Because of my writing about friendship I've ended up in a lot of conversations with asexual and aromantic people. As someone who has identified as allosexual and alloromantic — someone who does desire, value, and engage in relationships that include sex and romance — I at first thought this was just an odd quirk, that I'd written things that happened to resonate strongly with people in demographics and communities I don't belong to. Over the years I read and talked and learned more about the politics of asexuality and came to realize that there are many currents in asexual culture and values that deeply align with my own and that many ace folks have done a great deal of thinking and talking about things I've felt but not clearly articulated. In *Asexual Manifesto 2022*, Aley O'Mara writes, "A person does not need to 'be' asexual in order to practice a radical asexual politics."[2] It's been a great gift to learn from ace writers and thinkers.

A lot of Angela Chen's book *Ace* hinges on the question of how we differentiate types of relationships from one another. It turns out that when we take seriously the experiences and relationships of asexual and aromantic people, we also expose a profound ambiguity in what we consider conventional sexual and romantic relationships. I generally operate on the principle that we need to take people at their word about their own experiences and identities, not least because that is what I ask of others in my capacity as a trans person. So, it behooves us to believe asexual and aromantic people that a queerplatonic[3] relationship is something other than "just really good friends" or that a romantic relationship in which one or more people are asexual can be as meaningful and complete as any other.

Infatuation Plus Attachment

Chen cites a definition of romantic love as "infatuation and emotional attachment," which she attributes to the psychologist Lisa Diamond.[4] In the context of writing about asexuality, Chen is pointing out that this romantic love doesn't necessarily require sexual desire or sexual acts, that sex and romance tend to get conceptually squished up together but that it need not be so. That a relationship includes or has included infatuation, passionate depth of feeling, and/or sex tends to make us categorize it as a relationship that either is romantic, should be romantic, or would be romantic if those involved were honest and acting in good faith. But it's worth teasing apart infatuation, emotional attachment, sex, non-sexual physical intimacy, commitment, and other components of intimate relationships to investigate the many ways we can combine them.

C.S. Lewis, best known for the Narnia novels, wrote in an influential essay on friendship in his 1960 book *The Four Loves*, that in comparison to other types of love, friendship "has the least commerce with our nerves; there is nothing throaty about it; nothing that quickens the pulse or turns you red and pale."[5] I have often been turned red and pale by a friendship, but when I am, I tend to run into questions of category: is it really still friendship? If you work from a definition where friendships aren't passionate, but then encounter people in a friendship they experience as full of emotional depth, ardour, or infatuation, you will have to either rethink your conception of friendship or conclude that those friends are actually secretly dating or pining romantically for each other.

I sometimes hear people in longstanding friendships describe their relationship as being "like an old married couple." It's taken as given that a marriage can move from a passionate love to a companionate love. An old married couple or the pair of friends that resembles them may not love each other passionately, and they may not be having sex, but their relationship contains a profound depth of feeling. They know one another deeply, for better or worse. At this point, any question of exiting the relationship is pretty much out of the picture; you're in it for life. I grew up with a concept of friendship as steadier and less intense than romance. But if pressed, people operating with these concepts of friendship and romance still acknowledge that friendship certainly can include a passionate depth of feeling or that romantic love can be steady and companionate.

Never "Just" Friends

Much, probably too much, has been made of the institution of the "Boston marriages" of the late 19th and early 20th century, where two white women lived together and shared their lives without the financial support of a male romantic partner (but generally with access to generational wealth of some kind). It's both tempting and fundamentally impossible to read current identities onto people who lived before those identities existed, like asking whether Shakespeare was "gay" when that term only acquired its current meaning in the 20th century. These identities do not express something inherent; they are simply a way of gathering a set of actions and feelings into a convenient shorthand. The idea of sexual orientation as a cohesive and enduring identity that unifies and gives meaning to the relationships and sexual acts in someone's life only came into being relatively recently in the West. People before then in this part of the world simply did not organize their lives that way, and there are and have been many other ways of sorting things out.[6] But when a contemporary person looks at a Boston marriage and wonders whether it was actually one that we'd call lesbian or queer, what we really want to know is, were they having sex? It's clear their lives were deeply intertwined and committed. But that's not usually the part that moves it out of the terrain of friendship for a contemporary reader.[7] You know that joke people make when archaeologists find two skeletons entwined, or historians find a cache of love letters between people of the same gender and it gets reported on as a friendship, and someone needs to show their sophistication by saying that, "actually, they were fucking"? I hate that joke.

I write love letters to lots of people: some I currently have sex with, some I used to have sex with, some I have never had sex with, some I'd probably have sex with if we both felt like it. The sex is simply not that relevant! I do not experience friendship and romantic love as discrete and mutually exclusive or even necessarily on a gradient or spectrum. The people I am having sex with are not necessarily the people who are closest to me. They are not necessarily the people who'd show up at my bedside if I were in the hospital. Sex can be one way to deepen a relationship between or among people, but so are travelling together, supporting one another through crises, living together platonically, and many other things. One of the limitations of friendship is that it's so firmly seen as secondary and less than — that describing someone as a friend, even if, as I do, you reject the language of "just friends," will still give other people the impression that they are someone you care less about and are less committed to than a person you are having sex with.

One perspective on friendship that I enjoyed because it came from a set of experiences very different from my own was Wesley Hill's *Spiritual Friendship: Finding Love in the Church as a Celibate Gay Christian*. The author is a Christian who believes that Christianity forbids gay sex and has thus chosen to be celibate. He gives a lot of information about the history in Christianity, especially in medieval monastic communities, of "committed, promise-bound friendships," where pairs of people formalized their friendships like a marriage.[8] He's also candid about his longing as a celibate person for friendships that are devoted and committed, where he won't be left behind when his friends decide to focus on their romantic and sexual relationships instead. The thing it reminded me of the most was conversations with queer friends who are interested in sex but not in romantic relationships, monogamy, or the couple form, and are worried that it means they will be treated as disposable and won't be taken care of when they need it.

A lot of people in my life have sex with their friends without seeing it as necessarily escalating the friendship or changing it into something else. I see this most often in friends who are gay men and/or in kink and BDSM communities. I love the way Gayle Rubin describes and accounts for this in the quotation that opens this chapter: there is so much beauty in the friendships that are formed in and around sexual practices that are niche, that are stigmatized, that require mentorship and guidance to do safely and well. The men Rubin describes offering themselves up in the fisting slings at the Catacombs and people who opt out of sex are both operating outside of an amatonormative framework, which would tell them to focus their energies on a single primary romantic and sexual relationship, placing friendships and other connections firmly in second place. This shared outsiderdom is why *PrudeMag* — a zine for and by "spinsters, asexuals, relationship anarchists, celibates, and many other people challenging sex-necessarism," edited by Twoey Gray, Rea Sweets, and Jaden Tsan — uses the slogans "Prude-slut solidarity/ Prude-slut simultaneity" and "Free by our yes, free by our no." Outside the closed circle of the couple, prudes, sluts, and other conscientious objectors are joining hands and forging unique, bespoke relationships.

Making Friendship Legible

There are infinitely many possible clues people can use to guess another person's gender. People read gender onto another's body based on things like their height, their body shape, the pitch of their voice, the way they speak, the length and style of their hair, the presence or absence of facial and body hair, the type and style of clothes they are wearing, the materials their clothes are made of, if they are wearing jewellery and what kind, their name, and so on. When you look at someone you probably take in all of these things and, in an instant, weigh them against one another to guess their gender, with varying degrees of certainty depending both on how internally consistent their gender presentation seems to you and on the way other people in your life do gender.

If you feel dissatisfied with your own experience of gender and the way people in the world gender you, you can independently play with most of these variables. You can change your clothes, your hair, the name you go by, and the way you speak; you can take exogenous hormones and get surgeries to change the way your body looks, sounds, and smells. You can wear a hat or stop wearing hats. When you push any of these levers, you can see how they feel to you and also how they affect how other people read you.

I'm a transmasculine person in that I inject myself with testosterone every Wednesday. But "masculine" is a real stretch: I also have long hair, and I like silly earrings and florals and lace. I am not a man, and I don't particularly have an internal sense of gender identity. When I am with my friends, I dress however like. They know me, they know some things about my experiences and identities, and I trust them to believe that however someone describes their own gender is the final truth of the matter. I don't really worry about whether the gender signals I'm throwing are internally consistent or communicate a clear, legible gender identity. However, most people I encounter who don't know me are just trying to quickly decide whether to "sir" or "m'am" me. They may well be working with only two gender categories in which people can be placed, even though they understand that people within those categories can look a range of ways. When strangers read me as "probably a man (low degree of certainty), definitely fruity, homosexual of some kind," I feel more or less correctly gendered. When I put on too many femme signifiers, people may read me as a large woman with a deep voice, sometimes specifically as a trans woman. When I start getting read more consistently as a woman for a while, I flip a few gender switches in the other direction until the mix of ways people interpret me is more to my liking. But fundamentally I jump back and forth from the man box to the woman box in the eyes of people who only have those two boxes at their disposal.

This is how I also think of friendship and its place among other widely recognized types of relationships. Between you and someone you love, you can choose among any types of intimacy you want to include in or exclude from your relationship: emotional closeness, depth of conversation and disclosure, living together, sex, nonsexual physical intimacy, raising kids, sharing resources, and so on. You can include any combination of these things, and you can also call the relationship whatever you want. Having a lot of long conversations and cuddling but never fucking, and you call it a romantic relationship? That's allowed. Raising kids with a friend? You can do that. Hooking up with your coworker? Probably a bad idea but you can make your own choices.

Within your friend group or subculture there will be a range of types of relationships that are legible and recognized. If you hang out with ace people, you will probably know people in queerplatonic relationships. People in your life will have a sense of the ways a relationship like that tends to look, and if you are in a relationship like that it will make sense to them. But when you venture out into a broader world constructed along a romantic/platonic binary, people will not necessarily understand your queerplatonic relationship. They will want to know whether you're *really* friends or dating if those are the only two boxes available to them. And you will have to decide whether, how, and when to explain the nuances of your relationship to someone versus when you'd rather just pass as a type of relationship they understand.

Cultural models and expectations change, and they change by people doing things otherwise than they've been done. You might be willing to have a weird freaky unintelligible relationship, and your binary-breaking relationship might be strong enough and work well enough for you to weather constantly running afoul of expectations. There is so much joy and beauty in defying expectations and making your own thing, but it's also hard. It will probably take more explicit negotiation than you might want, and your relationship may flounder despite your values and your best efforts.

The Price of Ambiguity

In my closest friendships it is sometimes easy between the two of us for things to be ambiguous and fluctuating, to leave open the possibility of more care, more commitment, more touch, and more enmeshment than the strictures of friendship allow. What is hard is navigating the skepticism of others and their desire to situate the relationship somewhere fixed and specific. Surely we're secretly dating, or one or both of us wants the relationship to jump to a "romantic" steady state? Friendship is a flexible relationship surrounded on all sides by more rigid ones, and when it wriggles too close to one of them, people are going to prod at it and dissect it, and it may not survive those investigations.

I have a history of intense friendships, friendships that are the primary relationship in my life, friendships that are passionate and committed and that walked right up to the edge of being romantic relationships, where we talk a lot about rejecting arbitrary distinctions between friendship and romantic relationships. And those relationships that troubled the distinction between straightforward friendships and romantic relationships have been the ones that ended most badly. I'm friends with almost all of my romantic exes, but the most intractably hard feelings in my life are between me and people I'd been in close, intense, committed friendships with — friendships that looked and felt in some ways like romantic relationships. Those relationships ended in part like any others, because of incompatibilities between me and the other people in them that we couldn't or wouldn't reconcile. But I believe they were also squeezed to death between friendship and romance when they failed to resolve definitively in either direction. My ill-fated friendships were with, respectively, someone with a monogamous partner, a straight man, and someone who identified mostly as aromantic, and so there was danger for them in loving me too tenderly. Even though these friends and I talked explicitly about our desire to live out our feelings another way, or with looseness and flexibility, everybody in our lives wanted to know if we were secretly fucking. And we obviously loved each other, but were we *in love*? Having to navigate these questions was a source of constant tension in these in-between relationships. Sometimes I imagine these relationships as delicate, nebulous amoebas roving over the hard, sharp edges of categories. They could maybe have rested more peacefully within the bounds of one of those categories but snagged and tore on their edges.

Maybe these ambiguous romantic friendships also blew up in part because they combined the intensity of romance with friendship's lack of script. The scripts that govern romance and shape our conceptions of what a romantic relationship looks like do not, for the most part, serve us very well. They are deeply misogynistic, modelled on property contracts, full of judgement around sexuality, and a lot of other bad stuff. But they do serve as a common reference point around which we can organize some of our most intense feelings toward other people. They give us a framework for talking through those feelings and how to act on them with other people in our lives — both romantic partners and those outside the relationship. Even when we reject them, they give us something to react against: a negative space that we can decide how to fill.

This comes back to the ambiguity of friendship. Two people might consider themselves to be in a friendship while having very different understandings of what that means. People also tend to have more friendships, both concurrently and over the course of our lives, so you have more points of reference and potentially more understanding that one friendship can't meet all your needs and shouldn't be expected to.

THREE

Weaving Networks of Friendship

> [New York's] greatest offering to gays is friendship … For many people it has taken the place of love. Sex is casual, romance short-lived; the real continuity in many people's lives comes from their friends. Some advocates of friendship would argue that to receive sustenance from a dozen men and women is better than to pair off with just one other person, from whom one expects too much and receives too little.
>
> —EDMUND WHITE, *States of Desire: Travels in Gay America*[1]

I've been surprised to learn that friendships are apparently widely agreed to be relationships between two people. The Britannica definition tells us that friendship "is a dyadic relationship, meaning that it involves a series of interactions between two individuals known to each other … The fact that friendships are dyadic relationships distinguishes them from cliques or peer groups."[2] This is interesting to me because it's at odds with what I think of as a good friendship. In my own experience the best friendships are ones that are heavily networked.

Not long after they moved to Montreal and began to transition, my friend River became mysteriously, severely ill. Eventually they needed surgery and received medical care so violently transphobic that they nearly bled out overnight in the hospital because staff refused to touch them. They were estranged from their family of origin, unpartnered, and new in town. They had a smattering of not-yet-very-close local friends and few specifically trans friends. They describe the feeling of both coming out as trans and becoming chronically ill as encountering "multiple levels of sudden and mounting alienation between me and everyone I knew. It felt like an experience of extreme precarity and aloneness. I had these, in retrospect, pretty thin relationships that were tested, and most of them didn't survive."

Looking back on this time, River recalls their desperation in calling on relatively new friends to provide life-saving help. People found it easy to assume they had someone else, a parent, a partner, someone else who would be there, but they didn't. The experience has shaped the way they think about care, particularly among people who are outside of romantic and familial relationships. Specifically, it made them aware of the perils of thinking of friendships as a series of one-on-one dyadic relationships rather than as part of a network. With some chagrin, they describe their experience using the metaphor of defined contribution and defined benefit pensions.

In a "defined contribution friendship," you decide what you are willing and able to put in, and that's the end of your responsibility. If your friend is sick, maybe you can drop off some juice, but if they need a ride to the hospital and you don't have a car, they're out of luck. In a "defined benefit friendship," you orient less toward what you are personally able to do. Instead, you figure out what needs to happen. Your friend is going to be in the hospital for a while, and someone needs to be there every day. Probably no one person could or should be there every day, but someone needs to be. Instead of assessing what you individually can and can't do, or how much you are willing to give, you orient toward how you can work collectively to solve the problem and meet the need. As River put it:

> It's not functional to have all of these individualized relationships with people when you're in crisis. In cases of big needs, it typically doesn't add up to enough or doesn't add up to the right things. You have to get all of your serious needs met, and it doesn't need to be from any one person, but people need to make sure it happens. There was one friend who was into being bossy and arranging people, and it saved my life and also saved me psychologically. I think that kind of structure is also what makes it possible for everyone to have healthy and reasonable boundaries [about what they can offer].

The problem with the couple form, as it appears in monogamous relationships, is fundamentally that it concentrates way too many things in one relationship. But I think that this problem also shows up in a different guise in friendships: we tend to consider each of our relationships in isolation rather than as threads in a greater whole, connecting everyone involved to, ultimately, everyone else in the world.

When our friendships are dyadic and separate from one another, we are more inclined to think of what we can each individually offer rather than in terms of convening and coordinating people and making sure the inevitable gaps get filled. The coordinator also needs to not be the person receiving the care: it is much better for someone else to be the person hearing any no's and equivocation and flakiness. It can be hard enough to accept care without dealing with those aspects, so insulating the care recipient from them is a great gift.

I'm not personally accustomed to handling my relationships in this way. If someone has a need I can fulfill, I do so to the best of my ability. If they have a need I can't fulfill, I probably just do an amount I can and abdicate responsibility. In this way we are mostly left with big unfulfilled needs, especially those of us who don't have romantic or familial relationships to fall back on. When one of your friends needs more care than they are getting and more than you can easily provide, it's hard to reach out to other people and coordinate. It's hard because, at least in the circles I spend time in, it's not a very established phenomenon that I already have scripts for. I don't necessarily seek to know or have contact information for my friends' friends in a way that would allow me to readily shift into coordinating care and support for a friend if I needed to. It's harder to muster people when it is or feels like an emergency, and it feels easier to me to just push through it and do it all.

And the impulse to do it all yourself can be compelling! It is especially so if you are motivated by a desire to prove that you are special and worthwhile and indispensable — if you feel that you have to work to earn love. Maybe you think the harder you work the more love you can earn and the safer you will be. At some level I think that if I hoard all the work, maybe I can also hoard its presumed rewards; if people see how far I'm pushing past my limits, they will recognize that I deserve love. This rampant individualism can serve you well in some domains of life. It tends to work well in jobs. It *can* secure you some love and safety, at least sometimes, and for a while. But it does not serve the people you love, and it cannot protect you from rejection or loneliness.

One of my greatest joys in friendship is to be able to introduce my friends to one another, to meet new people through my friends, and to feel that I am woven into a social fabric that expands ever outwards. Growing older, and especially growing older in subcultures, means that many of the people in my life will have relationships and experience with each other going back decades. Sometimes this is fraught and inconvenient, and often it is a source of delight, insight, and funny stories.

Friendships are simply easier when they are not one-to-one relationships, even if everyone involved has a wealth of other one-to-one relationships. I am always grateful when a friend asks for help within a group chat and whoever in there has a free moment or insight into the dilemma they're facing can reply. They are assured of a response, but the friend who isn't checking their phone at that moment or doesn't know what to say can know that it's covered. I like being able to ask my friends — where appropriate — for advice about one another or to relay when someone is having a hard time and could use some care. One of my greatest joys in life is when someone I know is looking for a particular expertise I don't possess and I am able to connect them with another person in my life who does.

In *The Four Loves*, C.S. Lewis describes friendship as "a relation between men [sic] at their highest level of individuality. It withdraws men from collective 'togetherness' as surely as solitude itself could do; and more dangerously, for it withdraws them by two's and three's."[3] It's not controversial to say that romantic pairings often turn people in toward one another when they were previously oriented more out toward their wider networks. But I was surprised when I read C.S. Lewis's claim that he sees friendship working similarly, turning us inward toward one or two close relationships to the exclusion of a broader public. I think that friendship contains impulses both to turn inward toward one another and to turn outward toward the world, but personally I especially love when friendships pull me back toward the collective togetherness and turn me to face the broader world: introducing me to people, places, activities, and ideas I might never have found or warmed to otherwise.

Whether you think of it as an interwoven network or as a series of one-on-one relationships, friendship is a model of multiplicity and nonexclusivity in relationships. In *PALS*, I wrote that I love how in friendship, I find it easier to reject the principle of scarcity than I do in romantic relationships, and that "we can have many best friends and enjoy and be comforted by the fact that our best friends themselves have many best friends, spinning a globe-spanning web of inside jokes, late night phone calls and fierce, complicated loyalties, and in so doing showing us how much love we can hold."

There is so much I appreciate about friendship being a type of relationship that it is normative to have many of. When I need advice, have exciting news to share, or saw something funny, I always feel grateful when I scroll the list of friends in my phone and know that I have many people in my life and can choose the ones best suited to the occasion. My friends represent a wealth of different sets of experiences and areas of expertise. My relationships with them vary in depth, tone, and degrees of trust. The things we have in common with one another vary. I have friends who share aspects of my experience and identity, like being Quaker, having grown up rurally, being a white person who is critical about whiteness, being out as trans for over a decade, or being an avid reader. I also have friends whose experiences are completely different from my own with regard to any given aspect of my identity, and that is equally precious to me. The multiplicity of friendship is also important when something is going wrong in one of your other relationships. It means there are more likely to be witnesses: someone to notice that something is awry, someone for you to check in with — "This doesn't feel right: am I overreacting?"

The Danger of Dyads

When we think of friendships as a type of relationship that it is normal to have many of, it puts them into immediate contrast with monogamous romantic relationships. But when we think of friendships as a series of one-on-one dyads, even if any given person takes part in a lot of dyadic friendships, those relationships bear a lot of similarity to monogamous romantic relationships, including some of the difficulties associated with those.

When I spoke to my friend Julie about friendships, one of the first things they mentioned was that "abuse happens in dyads." This idea immediately resonated with me. I have found it all too easy to mould myself to the way someone wants or expects me to be in a relationship and wind up straying far from the ways I'd like to be or for my relationships to be. The only thing that helps recalibrate those norms is to talk it through with other people in my life. Too often I've described a situation that seems fine to me and have only realized it's not when I see someone else's reaction to it. Ultimately, I think friendships that happen in intense pairings, where two people are deeply turned inwards toward each other, have more in common with romantic pairings than they do with relationships that take place in a network. Relationships benefit from having more eyes on them, more people to weigh in when things go sideways. I think it's not only abuse that happens in dyads but also disappointment and resentment. The point isn't that relationships should never get weird or hard or fall into a crummy pattern, it's that we need help pulling them back to where we want them to be.

There is such a different feeling to my friendships that are interconnected with one another than to my friendships that are on islands of two, disconnected from the rest of my life. When I'm confused, annoyed, or hurt by someone's behaviour, it's tremendously helpful to be able to check in with someone else who knows them. And I also want this for my friends whenever I confuse, annoy, or hurt them. More networked friendships also let us call on more resources. Sometimes this is simply time and energy. When I don't have it in me to give a friend the care they need, I love knowing that someone else is there to step in. Other times I appreciate knowing that my friends can access types of skills and experience that I don't have — something specific to a cultural background I don't share, a subculture I don't know about, a type of dynamic I haven't experienced.

What does this look like in practice? At the simplest level, I love being in group chats with my friends. When someone wants to talk through a problem, if I'm not at my phone, someone else might be. When they make a joke I don't get, someone else will laugh. When their actions are concerning, someone else is seeing it, and I can check in with them to talk through how we might respond. There is something special to me about friend groups. I think it gets at what people observe about how different friendships in adulthood often feel from friendships in childhood, adolescence, and young adulthood. As children and younger people, we're more likely to be in groups of friends, and as we get older, these groups of friends can often disintegrate into pairings. This isn't universally true, of course: it depends on which of the conditions that create friend groups remain present in your adult life. Although they're not as ready-made as when you're a child, you can create these conditions any time in your life. In Part 3 of this book, I write about how, at a larger scale and a greater degree of organization, networks of friendship can morph into affinity groups, clubs, cohousing arrangements, and circles of mutual support and care.

Why We Let Our Friends Down

There are also difficult things about the assumed multiplicity of friendship. You might have a particular friendship as the central relationship in your life, but your friend may have a more diffuse circle of care, and the gap between your expectations can be painful. Knowing that people generally have a multiplicity of friends means less pressure on each of them. But it also means that it's easy to assume somebody else will be there for your friend. I wrote earlier about how much my idealistic view of friendship was tarnished when I asked friends to help me out after top surgery, and they mostly bailed and my romantic partner was stuck doing most of my care. Many years later, while talking to a friend about this, they pointed out, "People probably bailed *because* they knew you had a partner. They knew someone would be there, so they let themselves off the hook." In this case they were correct. My then-partner did care for me. She did a wonderful job, and I will always be grateful to her for it.

But it is also easy for people to assume that they do not have a strong obligation to a friend in need because surely somebody else is there. Especially insofar as your friendships are dyadic, one-on-one relationships and not strongly networked with others, we have less clarity about whom someone else has in their life to rely on. Having a lot of friendships means less pressure on each of them. But also under the WASP-centric, relatively attenuated definition of friendship that we know is culturally specific, it means it is easy for us to shrug off any sense of responsibility toward a friend. This comes back to the ambiguous, undefined nature of friendship that we talked about earlier, which has left many people in my life yearning for closer, more deeply enmeshed friendships: the type that shade into family.

FOUR

The Families We Choose

> Anyone who ever let me in his body or arms I still feel grateful to. That's why so many of my friends are old lovers, I suppose. And that includes, these days, dying and dead friends as well, to whom the flesh, my flesh, still connects me.
>
> —EDMUND WHITE, *The Beautiful Room Is Empty*[1]

It's probably a bad idea to get any ideas about life or about groups of people from reality TV. Nevertheless, when my queer friends and I watch shows like *Love Is Blind* and see the relationships that the straight contestants have with their families of origin, we often end up texting each other: Is this for real? Norms like asking permission from a partner's parents to marry them are unimaginable to me. I love my family, fortunately. Many of my friends love theirs; many others are estranged. But regardless, most of us place more emphasis on our "chosen family." The association of the term "chosen family" with queer friendships is so common that it's easy to take for granted. But once I started interrogating the cultural and subcultural concepts of friendship in my life, I became increasingly curious about the idea of chosen family and specifically what it has to do with 2SLGBTQ+ identities. It seemed self-evident to me that the hope and weight I put into my friendships has much to do with being gay and trans, but why?

In the introduction to his book *Gay Mens' Friendships: Invincible Communities*, Peter Nardi writes that many gay men have told him "how important their friends are to them, how this 'rich network of friends' is like a family, how sex has been a dimension of their earlier friendships with some of their friends, and how, for some, their friends mean more and last longer than do their romantic relationships."[2] This is my experience as well. The queer people in my life are not necessarily better friends than straight people, but we tend to think and talk a lot about friendship and hold it close to our hearts.

Chosen Family Hits the Mainstream

The term "chosen family" entered wide parlance after the 1991 publication of *Families We Choose: Lesbians, Gays, Kinship* by Kath Weston, a white lesbian academic. In her 1997 preface to the book's paperback edition Weston asks, "After I began fieldwork in San Francisco in the mid-1980s … All around me, people had begun talking about something called 'gay families,' the 'families we choose.' … Why were lesbians and gay men busy recasting close friends as kin?"[3] In 80 interviews in the San Francisco Bay Area conducted between 1985 and 1987, Weston looks at what gays and lesbians mean when we talk about friends as chosen family, as well as other gay and lesbian experiences of family, such as coming out to their families of origin, becoming parents, and how people conceptualize their sense of their sexual identity and their relationships with their families in concert with other aspects of their identity, like race, class, and religion. Not all friends are chosen family. Weston found that some of the factors that make someone more likely to consider a friend family include "offers of assistance, commitment to 'working through' conflicts, and a common history" — essentially, commitment to sticking around and being there for each other.[4]

The most obvious answer to why queer people would be more likely to build families out of our friendships is that so many of us have experienced rejection, abuse, or violence from our families of origin or have had those families simply decline to know us for all that we are. If the family you grew up with is shitty, maybe you'll try and find a new one. But Weston found that whether a gay or lesbian person had been disowned by their family of origin didn't correlate strongly with whether they formed a chosen family or how much they valued their chosen kin. And those who reconciled with their families of origin didn't value their chosen families any less. Those of us with loving or at least cordial relationships with our families of origin are inevitably in community with others who were thrown out of their homes, subjected to conversion therapy, or experienced other forms of abuse from the families they grew up in. Most any group of queer people will include at least some people whose family of origin was awful to them. Maybe community norms have just grown to accommodate that.

Google Books' Ngram Viewer, which tracks the prevalence of a word or phrase in its indexed books, begins to show usage of the phrase "chosen family" after 1940: there is a small initial bump around World War II, then very little usage until around 1980, when it begins to accelerate, dramatically speeding up around 2005.[5] People have been considering others as family those who they are not related by blood or marriage since time immemorial; there are countless longstanding traditions by which people not in a romantic relationship to one another can become each other's family. But the particular term "chosen family" has had an interesting trajectory. The first published uses I could find of the term are all from a Christian context, referring to believers as the chosen family of Christ,[6] but it wasn't a widely used term until the 1980s.

I have a suspicion that, like many things regarded as part of "queer culture" writ large, a lot of ideas of chosen family originated in culturally specific racialized, especially Black, queer communities and the general idea of them made its way outwards minus the cultural specificity and the context that made it work. I found one fascinating usage of "chosen family" in the minutes of a 1973 meeting of the US House of Representatives Committee on Internal Security, on "Revolutionary Activities Directed Toward the Administration of Penal or Correctional Systems," or what I would call prison abolition activism.[7] It is a fascinating report that inadvertently preserves precious documentation of abolitionist organizing while testifying to the depth of surveillance placed on largely Black organizers who were incarcerated or working in solidarity with incarcerated people at a time when the US was about to expand the number of people it imprisoned to six times its 1974 levels over the following 20 years.[8]

Within the more than 1,400 pages of this report is the document "Our Family's Role and Ideology," written by the Black

Guerilla Family (BGF), a Black Marxist-Leninist prison gang whose co-founders included George Jackson and which remains active to this day.[9] Jackson was one of the "Soledad Brothers" charged with the murder of a correctional officer in 1970. The same year he published a memoir that became a bestseller and a touchstone of Black Power politics. The following year, he was killed by guards during an escape attempt and became a martyr within Black liberationist circles. The BGF manifesto contains the sentence, "We are the brothers who, in reality are a chosen family of comrade George Jackson, instead of one 'George Jackson,' we are many." If your reference point for the concept of chosen family is something more like a wholesome young adult novel, you will find this vision of chosen family pretty different. The next sentence states, "We are the brothers who will dish out vicious and strategic moves within the confines of the concentration camps wherever injustice is perpetrated against the BGF or its members." It is an unquestionably material and political concept of chosen family.

Chosen families likewise structure the Black and Latinx 2SLGBTQ+ subculture of ballroom. The lineage of ballroom can be traced back to drag balls held in the mid-19th-century United States by performers like William Dorsey Swann, who was born into slavery in Maryland.[10] Ballroom began to emerge in its contemporary form in the middle of the 20th century when racialized drag performers carved out a space where they could find reprieve from the racism of white-dominated drag communities. It's customary for ballroom performers to organize themselves into houses, where older and more experienced performers mentor younger ones, often providing housing, care, and material support as well as artistic guidance. In his book *And the Category Is…: Inside New York's Vogue, House, and Ballroom Community*, Ricky Tucker beautifully pays tribute to these families:

> At its core Ballroom is an answer to an act against nature: parents disowning their children ... These are the people meant to protect you from cruelty and to love you unconditionally, not to be the source of your greatest trauma. This kind of excommunication plays out on a cellular level, your nervous system triggered any time someone henceforth tries to get close to you. Your self-worth is often mixed up in it and constantly in question, a feeling understandably commensurate with how sexually desirable you feel, because desire is what got you here in the first place. Your light is dimmed, your body branded. No. It's not societal; it's biological. And when Mother Nature sees a vacuum, she fills it.[11]

This is family in a literal, material sense. I love the way Tucker recontextualizes the concept of a "biological" family to refer to one that is not related by blood but that responds to a nervous-system-level need for love and stability. To me it's the clearest articulation of what is meant by chosen family.

It's unlikely that white people like me would know much of anything about ballroom without the 1990 documentary *Paris Is Burning*, directed by the white lesbian filmmaker Jennie

Livingston. In her book *Black Looks: Race and Representation*, bell hooks criticizes Livingston's relationship to the people and culture she depicts, her "cultural arrogance," and her lack of "awareness of the way white supremacy shapes cultural production."[12] I don't claim any authority to decree who makes movies about whom, but I also don't watch *Paris Is Burning* without an awareness that it represents a white person's view of a Black and Latinx art form and subculture. In the 35 years since it came out, *Paris Is Burning* has continued to capture the imagination of people worldwide. It has, for better or worse, travelled far beyond the milieu it depicts. The scene *Paris Is Burning* depicts, and the way it depicts it, has had a strong influence on queer cultures writ larger and whiter. White people are famously not very good at understanding that there are things in the world that are not about or for us. I also think it's easy to mistake awareness that something exists, and a desire for it, for having it, or for even having the preconditions for having it. I think that in some cases, white middle-class queers like myself know about chosen family, yearn for chosen family, and have convinced ourselves that we have it, even if we don't materially or culturally know how to be in that type of relationship.

Weston suggests that structures of chosen family are perhaps remarkable (and worthy of a special name) insofar as they represent whiter and more middle-class people taking on family structures that might be normal among their friends who are racialized and/or grew up poor or working class. Specifically, she writes that the chosen families of the Bay Area queers she talked to, regardless of their race and class, looked more like the bonds among "African-American, American Indian [as in Indigenous], and white working class" communities.[13] The concept of chosen family may also have voyaged across class lines. Weston found that when her interviewees considered someone family, they would be more likely to exchange material support, like money, with one another. She points out, citing the anthropologist Rayna Rapp, that usually in the US, middle-class people tend to share emotional support but less often material support.[14] But Weston observed queer people of a variety of class backgrounds and statuses helping their friends out with money.

In some kinds of queer spaces, white queer people raised middle class will come to share space with people of different cultural and class backgrounds, more so than they might if they were straight. Through meeting, being around, and building friendships and romantic relationships with people who are racialized and/or working class, middle-class white queers may well come away with different values than we had before. One of these might be a greater sense of duty to materially care for the people in our lives. That is a good thing, I think! I'm not arguing that white people or middle-class people are doing something wrong when we build families of choice or describe our closest friendships as such. I think it just might be the case that we only consider it something special when it's us who are doing it. Words, concepts, styles, and art forms moving from culturally and subculturally specific Black usage to broader white usage is a common phenomenon, and not a neutral one. I think it behooves us at least to be curious about where the concepts we're mobilizing come from and how our relationship to them differs from that of the communities where they originated.

However, I have a suspicion that sometimes what happens is that middle-class white people like me come into community with people whose norms include a much stronger sense of duty to other people and we absorb the language that surrounds it, like "chosen family," but don't necessarily have the skills and reflexes to back it up. I believe in the importance of showing up for the people in my life when they are in need, even when I'm tired and already stretched too thin and that person is annoying. But I am so much worse at that than most of my friends who are racialized and/or were raised poor or working class. Those are the friends I see showing up over and over for members of their families of origin even when they're sick of that person's bullshit. If I am any good at showing up it is because I have tried, consciously and imperfectly, to learn from them. I think that what a lot of us have is a chosen-family-shaped hole in our hearts and lives. We know about it, we value it, we want it, but we don't really know what it looks like or how to get there. We may even think we have it, then get our feet knocked from under us when it doesn't materialize in our time of need. Why do we fail to show up for one another, and how we can do otherwise?

AIDS and Queer Family

Best known for the work of articulating the ways that that institutional power flows through every corner of our lives, gay theorist Michel Foucault turned his attention to friendship toward the end of his life. I wish he had had more time to think through friendship and to see and speak to the fullness of the changes that occurred in queer communities throughout the 1980s, but he died of AIDS in 1984. In a 1982 interview, Foucault argued that what straight people feared most about gays was that we would "develop relationships that are intense and satisfying even though they do not at all conform to the ideas of relationship held by others ... the prospect that gays will create as yet unforeseen kinds of relationships that many [straight] people cannot tolerate."[15] Decades later, have we ended up developing types of relationships so different and beautiful that heterosexuals tremble in fear? Probably not, but I do see my queer friends working hard to build lives that value and prioritize friendship more deeply than it is in the templates many of us grew up with.

I don't think it's possible to overstate the importance of AIDS in shaping the concept and importance of queer chosen family. As people sickened and died, and buried and grieved their friends, they needed the kind of intensive, hands-on, non-negotiable care that other people might be able to expect from their families of origin or from institutions like hospitals and hospices. But AIDS emerged in a world where many people experienced profound homophobia (as well as transphobia, racism, whorephobia, and stigma against drug use) in both their families of origin and the institutions that were supposed to care for them. It fell on friends to take up work and roles that were more intimate and demanding than friendship might otherwise have included.

Chosen family can encompass and blend both deep friendships among adults and the kinds of caretaking relationships between adults and children that are more commonly associated with family.

When my friend Hannah, a white cis queer woman in her 30s, decided she wouldn't have children of her own, she feared that she would be lonely and uncared for when she was old, even though she doesn't believe that people necessarily have an obligation to provide elder care for their parents and knows it doesn't always happen. Suddenly, though, she realized that being alone would be at odds with the life she's built for herself. It struck her that she has consistently been able to create community and family for herself that is not based on blood: "Why would that go away once I hit a certain age? I'm probably not going to be alone in the end of my life. It probably won't be children and grandchildren, but I'll still have community." In that moment, she realized that despite her own strongly held values around friendship and community care, she had still internalized narratives that people who don't have one longstanding romantic partner and biologically related children will die alone. Taking a look at the life she'd built for herself, one filled with close friendships, helpful neighbours, and kids who consider her an aunt despite their lack of genetic connection, she realized that "have kids" versus "die alone" is a false dichotomy.

Chosen Family as an Ideal

From the beginning of my skepticism about whether friendship could or should play the role in my life that I yearned for it to, I have kept returning to the term "chosen family." It seems to group together a lot of intense, unexamined desires, and I consider it ground zero for the conceptual vagueness around friendship, family, community, and related concepts. In the mostly queer and trans circles I run in, I often see friendship held up as a domain where we can be loved and known and cared for in a way that avoids the pitfalls of both conventional romantic relationships and our families of origin. We yearn for love that lies outside of relationships of power and domination. We often seek that love in our friendships and bring to our friendships the hope that they will be exempt from the same structures of violence and power that have shaped every other intimate relationship we've had. The idea of friendship as a space outside of relations of power goes back, in the Western tradition, at least as far as Aristotle. Friendship is a bond based on care and one we enter into more or less voluntarily and can leave more readily than many other kinds of relationships. Held up against familial relationships and heteronormative romantic relationships, friendship seems egalitarian. I think it's worth looking at to what extent that's true.

An absence of power is part of the fantasy of friendship. But in practice, friendship, like every other type of relationship and human activity, takes place in a world shaped by unequal power. Any relationships between two or more people will take place, in some way or another, across differentials of power and privilege. Chosen family is a term that seems to describe an ideal: one whose reality in our lives is up for debate. It expresses, to me, the fantasy that friendship could give us the love we desire from a family, without the hurt, betrayal, and abuse many of us experience in our families of origin. The fantasy is that, if we could choose the people who constitute our families, we could also pick and choose everything else about the relationship and could opt out of inequality, domination, betrayal, and abandonment. We can't, of course — not in our families of origin, not in our families of choice. The best we can do is to build our capacity for repair so that when things go wrong, we have a fighting chance of rebuilding them.

Queer people are notable for keeping our exes in our lives more than straight people do. Partly this is out of necessity: in a small subculture, people are more closely networked and there are simply not enough people, enough parties, enough gay bookstores, for us to avoid our exes even if we wanted to, which sometimes we definitely do. Generally, whenever someone has been important to me but our relationship has come apart, I try to eventually, even if it's over the course of decades, work my way back to having them in my life in at least a distantly cordial capacity. For the exes I've kept in my life, I feel resistant to calling them friends. I tend to keep referring to them as "my ex" even long after our romantic relationship ends because I feel that what we have is something other than friendship. I'm ambivalent about this, because it's possible that referring to someone as an ex and not a friend might convey ill will or the absence of a relationship, but I do it because I feel protective of a distinctive relationship with deep meaning to me. Sometimes I'll qualify it by saying "my cherished ex" or "my ex, who remains one of my favourite people." I wish there were an easier shorthand I could use to communicate this but maybe the word I mean is "family."

As one of Kath Weston's interviewees put it, "After you break up, a lot of people sort of become as if they were parents and sisters, and relate to your new lover as if they were the in-law."[16] At best, exes are people who know one another as well as anyone else in their lives, who have gone through a big rupture or change in their relationship, have very likely seen one another at their worst, and have, after all that, decided to stay in each other's lives. I bristle whenever people describe a romantic relationship as "more than friends." I don't buy into hierarchies among different types of relationships, and I wouldn't be writing a book about friendship if I didn't take it seriously. But if we're going to stick to that naming convention, maybe we should refer to the exes who are still in our lives as "more than partners."

In his book *Relationship Anarchy: Occupy Intimacy!*, Juan Carlos Pérez Cortés makes a provocative argument in favour of what I'd call "abolishing breakups." The "relationship anarchy" approach, as he defines it, includes the idea that "the fixed attitudes we currently have toward love on one hand and friendship on the other can be blended together and practiced naturally at each moment, depending on the circumstances."[17] In addition to undermining hierarchies among different relationship configurations, his hope is that this will allow relationships to change more organically over time without necessarily having to end when they only need to change. In this approach, if you no longer have romantic or sexual feelings for someone, you may be able to pause or discontinue those aspects of your relationship without having to throw away the parts that are still working. As Pérez Cortés puts it, "It's likely that you still have many other things to share with that person, above all love, affection, and the desire to care for each other." He argues that the pain of breakups comes in part from realizing there's a disjunction between what you desire from someone close to you and what they desire from you, but also from the arbitrary differences in status between romantic and non-romantic relationships. If we didn't see friendship as less important than coupledom or if we ceased to think of our connections as defined by those categories, breakups would hurt less.

Some relationships need to conclusively end, and some bridges are worth burning. Sometimes you have hurt each other so much that it becomes impossible to find the will or the path to repair, a way back to enjoying each other's company. Sometimes one or more of the people in the relationship change such that you can no longer fit into each other's lives. Sometimes people turn out to have values and preferences that are so different that you can no longer enjoy the things you do have in common. But many relationships are worth keeping and honouring as they shift and change over months, years, decades.

Given that the word "family" already encompasses an incredibly broad constellation of relationships, I'm curious what we are trying to do by referring to friends as "chosen family." Nardi writes, "Friendship has its own structure and meanings in gay men's lives and does not need the metaphor of kinship to give it substance."[18] Maybe we sell friendship short and concede too much territory to family by naming our best and closest friendships as chosen family. Or maybe we should just be calling these relationships "family," full stop.

To me, "chosen family" is an ideal I point myself toward. Its appeal lies largely in what I wrote about in Chapter 3 — of having relationships that are interwoven, a crew of people who know each other deeply, a cluster of relationships that are greater than the sum of their parts. When I talked to my friend Imogen about friendship, one of the things she told me was that when she first started doing drugs one of the things she loved about them and that drew her in was the feeling of being part of a family: "I had this little crew of degenerate meth addicts and I was totally one of 'em. All we did was hang out and smoke meth and stay up all night and laugh our asses off and do weird shit." She told me that for her, a big part of the appeal of drugs was the built-in community: "If you're an outsider and you don't feel part of anything, doing drugs will immediately make you part of something." That sense of family proved short-lived for her: the connections dissipated as the members of that chosen family slipped deeper into use and she ended up homeless and isolated. She's now housed and in recovery but the memory of that short-lived sense of family still evokes strong feelings of grief in her. The feeling of family is important, and it's something many of us need more of in our lives.

HOW DO THE FRIENDSHIPS IN YOUR LIFE BECOME DEEPER AND STRONGER?

A combination of humour and silliness along with a willingness to talk about big/sometimes heavy topics, personal or existential. Spending time in person, on the phone, or on video call is the best way for me to deepen relationships. I love talking with people about anything and everything! I love playing in imaginary spaces, too.

— MARLAINA

Through shared experiences and talking about these experiences after. Connecting over art. With my best friend, we saw an exhibition we both deeply connected with, together, in the beginning of our close friendship, and that definitely deepened our connection. The exhibition was about queer friendships as well, so go figure.

— ERIN

Authenticity. For a long time I thought friendship meant moulding myself to what other people wanted, but that's not true. Friendship is about being the person you really are together with people who appreciate you for it — and appreciating them in kind. I'm an absurdly sentimental person; I'm so soaked in sincerity I fear I'm getting mouldy, a saturated washcloth in the corner of an old basin. But I'm not. I radiate it outwards and look for the people around me who welcome it and who reflect it. It condenses less like mould then and more like water vapour in the air on a summer day. Dew on new petals.

— CARA

PART TWO

WHY IS FRIENDSHIP SO HARD?

As I wrote in the preface to this book, my belief is basically that our friendships are not doing OK because we are not doing OK. On the face of it, this doesn't seem insightful or worth saying. But it felt worthwhile to write an entire book about this because it's something I've had trouble internalizing and have benefited from unpacking in detail. I am torn between a strong sense of personal responsibility on one hand and, on the other, a desire to place my individual choices within a larger context.

The Politics of Lonely is a made-up book the narrator is reading in the Weakerthans' song "(Hospital Vespers)" from their 2003 album *Reconstruction Site*. Despite having listened to the album hundreds times in the two decades it's been out, I didn't think much about its throughline of spending time with someone who is very sick in a hospital until I was listening to it while on my way to and from the hospital where someone I loved was very sick. It was October, then November, then December, and I was commuting to an out-of-the-way hospital from various locations all over a sprawling city that I did not live in, in clothes inadequate for the weather and increasingly stained and stinky, having packed for one week and stayed for many, exhausted and out of it and missing my stop over and over and over or taking the bus the wrong direction and ending up god knows where in the cold, with that album playing on repeat. "(Hospital Vespers)" is about trying to provide small moments of dignity to a person who is in the hospital, specifically by covering the security in their room so they can pray privately. Until this experience, I didn't realize the vigilance it takes to ensure that someone gets good care. Damn, what innocence to be well into my thirties and only just learning this, something many people learn much earlier and more harshly.

Even if the person who is hospitalized is, as my friend was, skilled at advocating for themselves, they will simply receive better care if they are able to prove by the presence of visitors that people outside of the hospital love them and are looking out for them. I wish it wasn't like that, but it seems that's how it is. I learned how vital it is to have someone to take notes about what is happening, what drugs and treatments someone receives and how they respond to them, when the person in the bed is unable to do so. I learned about how important it is that someone have access to supplies from the outside world: fresh pillowcases, gum, soda, non-hospital food. I learned how if you are tall and look like a man you can intimidate a shitty doctor into taking your friend's care seriously by doing almost nothing at all, just standing there. I will always be grateful for the chance to learn these things.

I have heard also from non-incarcerated people who support people in prison that sending mail to an incarcerated person is important not only to care for them but also to make it evident to guards that that person has friends outside who care about them and who would know if something bad happens to them. Demonstrating that a vulnerable person inside an institution is nevertheless part of a network of relationships outside provides a measure of protection against institutional violence and neglect. It is awful to realize the need to prove in this way that someone's life has value and to think about the many, probably the majority, of people who have no one outside to vouch for them in that way and are subject to whatever violence, neglect, or mercy institutions decide to serve up. Each of us needs a lot of people, and we need them very badly.

The season I spent commuting to the hospital made me think about the politics of lonely, what a less lonely politics might look like, and how differently we may have to do things to get there. I would always cite friendship as one of my core values and priorities, and during that time I put friendship at the centre of my life and got to see what it felt like to make friendship my full-time job. It was deeply meaningful and it also wrecked me. I felt crushed in the collision between the care the situation demanded and the ever-grinding infrastructure of capitalism. At the end of the day, I'd get Swiss Chalet from the cafeteria and eat for the first time, pulling off the mask I'd worn all day without eating or drinking because the ward was in a COVID outbreak. I'd sit on the bench outside the hospital and eat chicken and cry. I felt grateful that a large portion of the people in and around hospitals are in extremis and it's about as acceptable a place as you can find to eat ravenously in public and come visibly undone.

In not sharing the parts of the story that aren't mine to tell, I risk giving the impression that I consider myself to have been the main character of this experience. I understand that I was not, but I'll still speak only for and of myself here. It felt transcendent to be jarred out of routine: them so terrifyingly sick, me so far beyond tired, the way that hospitals seem to exist mostly outside the cycle of day and night and of passing months. You walk out and it's dark out now. You walk in and someone has put up a Christmas tree. I felt completely unmoored, tied only to my friend, who was floating in painkillers and pain. It was deeply meaningful and also exhausting in a way that I still carry in my body two years later. The experience made me aware of three things:

- It is important to me to be able to care for my friends when they need help. Work is important to me on a paying-the-rent level, but caring for the people I love is my actual priority.
- I can't do it alone. I'll want to try and take everything on myself and I can't. When someone needs care, there should be an abundance of people to care for them and outer circles of people caring for the carers.
- Like many people, I can't readily mobilize an abundance of structured care on short notice.

Why wasn't my life set up that way? Why was it so hard for me, someone who values friendship so much, to put friendship at the centre of my life, even temporarily? Our current friendship-dampening politics of lonely has many components, and in Part 2, I look at some of the structural factors that make friendship so hard and what we can do about them on the scale of our own lives.

Chapter 5, "The Ideology of Coupledom," examines how bureaucratic parts of life, like health insurance rules and job sick-leave policies, demonstrate a clear hierarchy of which relationships matter, and friendship rarely makes the cut. The material factors constraining who we can care for are real, but we always have a choice and can do things differently.

In Chapter 6, "Shredded Social Safety Nets," I dig into the question of why everything is so hard. The enshittification of social services, the erosion of collective institutions like labour unions, and our increasing social atomization can all be traced back to an ideology that has been consuming the world since the late 20th century.

Chapter 7, "Lonely, Expensive Homes," looks at how the cost and structure of our housing shape our social lives. In North America, housing is most people's largest expense, so when its cost grows much faster than our income, it plays an outsize role in constraining how we spend our days. How would our lives and friendships be different if our housing situations were cheaper and/or more communal and sociable?

In Chapter 8, "Work, the Joy-Eater," I describe how becoming a freelancer after many years of full-time in-person work woke me up to the possibility of moving work away from the centre of my life. Many people whose work situations changed in the early days of the COVID-19 pandemic also reassessed how work stood in the way of things they actually cared about. What can you do when the values you identify yourself with aren't reflected in the way you spend your time?

These are far from the only structural factors that make friendship difficult: others that I hope other writers will tackle include masculinity (how men and people perceived as men inherit constrained emotional and social ranges), ableism (how structural barriers to disabled people's full participation in social worlds forecloses their friendships), and a lack of resources for parents (how parents, especially primary caregivers of younger children, often lack access to supports that would allow them to maintain social lives). It is important to name and call out these structural issues, and it is equally important to imagine alternatives. I have been determined not to write a self-help book, because I believe that the message that you can fix all your problems on an individual level implies that they're your fault to begin with. My whole point here is that the configuration and timbre of our intimate lives are informed to a much greater extent by large structural forces than a lot of us tend to think. But while I don't believe that you can single-handedly wrest yourself out of history, I do think that there's worth in looking around and situating yourself, and that once you do there is some room to move. Our inability to imagine worlds based on interwoven relationships of mutual solidarity and care holds up a capitalist world order that depends on our being isolated, lonely, and desperate.

FIVE

The Ideology of Coupledom

> Your friends are your emotional support system, but you aren't allowed to ask them to consider your opinion in their plans, especially if you're the single person and the friend is in a couple. Why? Even two single friends who are close and derive companionship from each other are not supposed to consult each other and consider the other's feelings about big life decisions. If you are a big part of my emotional support and vice-versa, why is it not okay to ask for consideration?
>
> —AMEYA NAGARAJAN, *Yaari: An Anthology on Friendship by Women and Queer Folx*[1]

The vision of who you can care for, in what ways, and how much, is deeply embedded throughout laws, policies, and norms. No matter how good your intentions are about prioritizing friendship, you will come up against ideologies that specify which people are allowed to matter to you and how much. These ideologies don't just live in our hearts and minds but are also embedded in the structure and policies of the organizations that govern our lives.

At the beginning of the ongoing COVID-19 pandemic I was single and living alone in a bachelor apartment in Ottawa, Ontario. In what I had not yet known were the last years before the pandemic, I'd enjoyed living alone. I worked in an office, was in a loving long-term romantic relationship, and was constantly busy seeing friends and going to protests, events, and meetings for various projects and committees. Living alone was a pleasant reprieve from my busy people-filled life. You know what happened early in 2020. The job and projects all moved online. My relationship fell suddenly apart around the same time. In June 2021, the Ontario government recommended that people form "bubbles" or "social circles." "Think of your social circle as the people you can hug and touch, or those who can become part of your daily and weekly routines," a now-archived page on the government website advised. After the period in which people were asked not to have contact with anyone outside their household, social circles were a compromise designed for lonely singletons like me. Not having touched or shared a meal with another person in months, I was desperate to share space with other people. I had never been so cognizant of myself as an animal. Divorced from the physical proximity of others, I felt like if anything in my life went wrong, nothing and nobody stood between me and total ruin.

Waiting to see if I would be invited into anyone else's bubble filled me with dread. Fortunately, I was. A close friend had moved back in with her parents as the pandemic spread throughout North America and made her previously fairly chill job working at a grocery store one where she was now expected to put her life on the line for the same shitty pay as before. Their household invited me into their bubble. I was pathetically grateful and also aware that the invitation was contingent on their immediate family's needs as well as on the policy decisions of a Conservative government.

Living through 2020 and the first half of 2021, as a single person living alone who had set my life up around a wide net of relationships, rather than one household, made me aware at a bodily level that the way I had organized my time and my heart was outside of that which was expected of people, even though it truly did not seem that weird and freaky to me. I found that there were large and unforeseen consequences to organizing my life around friendship. To some extent I had known that the way I'd set my life up was unusual. I'd struggled with things like getting time off work when friends needed help. I've always gotten a sense that the jobs I work wanted me to only have two kinds of people in my life: my coworkers and a family (spouse-equivalent partner, parents, kids). Anyone more outside of that was unintelligible and risky.

The best description I have seen of how and why jobs constrain our personal lives is by Dr. Autumn BlackDeer, a queer decolonial scholar-activist from the Southern Cheyenne Nation, in a post she made on LinkedIn:

> In a capitalist society, your connections to community are a weakness. Need to leave early to pick up your kids? Total failure. Can't attend in-person meetings for taking your mom to a chemo appointment? Not committed to your career. Won't let us extract from your historically exploited community? Gatekeeping. They want you to be isolated, have no sense of self or outside connections; just be solely dependent upon success at work to define you and you'll do great.[2]

I had never felt so acutely burdened by the disjunction between the way my life was set up and the world's expectations of what a normal, valuable social world looked like. I don't think that people living as couples or in nuclear families were doing especially well either. Their experiences weren't easy, but they were the experiences that the government was expecting people to have.

At the same time as a very small collection of ways to organize your life were being held up as the only options, many people were realizing the paucity of those options and longing for alternatives. Interviewed in the spring of 2020 about her pandemic experiences, author and activist Naomi Klein wrote that while she'd spent her entire adult life living "alone, in a couple, or in a nuclear family," the early days of COVID made her rethink that. She realized that during "shocks that knock out our civic infrastructure" like COVID has, "single-family homes are a really bad technology." She observed that the people in her life who were weathering the crisis best were those who were living "in some kind of co-housing set up — with parents, kids, elders, and single people all living in connected spaces with a shared yard and communal areas" and sharing resources like "skills, childcare, and backyard vegetables."[3]

Writing in 2026, it's poignant to look back on spring 2020 as a moment when, amidst incalculable loss and social murder, possibilities and hopes also opened up. It feels like the intervening years have been nothing but a race back to a shitty status quo, but I remain hopeful that some of the seeds planted in that time are still germinating.

Unbundling Marriage

The ultimate way that dyadic forms of care are privileged over networked forms is through marriage. In US federal law alone there are "1,138 federal statutory provisions … in which marital status is a factor in determining or receiving benefits, rights, and privileges."[4] If you're lucky enough to have a job that allows for paid leave for caretaking or bereavement or that offers health insurance, these are benefits you're almost certainly only allowed to use within narrowly constrained notions of relationship and family. Everyone else is quitting jobs, getting fired, using vacation time, flexing their hours around if they're lucky enough to be able to do so, and putting that same $20 into each other's GoFundMes.

Thinking of the least expansive and visionary example possible, if you're signing up for insurance through a job, why can't you just choose one to four people who you want to be able to share your insurance with? Why do they have to be people who are in a specific legally defined relationship with you? Thinking more expansively, why can't everyone just have health benefits regardless of who does or doesn't claim them?

Earlier in this book, I talked about the concept of "amatonormativity" in the context of asexual and aromantic communities. While those communities adopted and expanded upon the term, it was originally coined by legal scholar Elizabeth Brake in her 2012 book *Minimizing Marriage: Marriage, Morality, and the Law*. The book examines the ways that marriage and relationships similar to marriage, like living with a monogamous romantic partner, are privileged over "the unpartnered and those in nontraditional relationships — quirkyalones, urban tribes, care networks, polyamorists — and same-sex partners, where they are prohibited from marriage."[5] Brake coined the term amatonormativity to describe this "focus on marital and amorous love relationships as special sites of value" over other ways of structuring one's life and relationships.[6]

Brake considers whether we'd be better off abolishing marriage altogether but ultimately argues for what she calls "minimal marriage," where people could "select from a greatly reduced set of the rights and responsibilities currently exchanged in marriage and to assign them to whomever they want, so long as the purpose is to support a caring relationship."[7] Essentially, marriage (and relationships that are legally equivalent or similar to marriage) bundle together a whole lot of things, including hospital visitation rights, entitlement to insurance benefits, and immigration and residency rights. Minimal marriage would unbundle these. Any or all of them could be given to an important romantic partner, but any could also be withheld. They could also be distributed more broadly among a wider group of people. Maybe your romantic partner is terrified of hospitals and not a good person to take charge of your care if you're unable to do so yourself. Maybe your best friend doesn't hold citizenship and you're willing to go through that awful process to vouch for them without having to fake a romantic relationship.

A few years ago, as someone with a deep interest in friendship and the ways we think and talk about friendship, I noticed a spate of interest in "platonic marriages" — friends with no past, current, or planned romantic relationship marrying one another. In a platonic marriage, the entire bundle is still given to one person, but it's just someone you don't necessarily kiss on the lips. I think a platonic marriage is more like a romantic marriage than anything else, in that you are still choosing one person to centre your life around. And a lot of marriages are platonic for many reasons: for example, it is not uncommon for spouses to stop having sex and for their relationships to shift into a more companionable state.[8] Platonic marriages sever the link between marriage and romance on an individual basis while maintaining the link between benefits and marriage on a social basis.

Fundamentally, though, I'd rather live in a world where everyone has access to the benefits marriage confers, no matter how the people they love and are loved by are configured in their life, or whether they have any close relationships at all. As long as insurance plans dictate what kind of relationship you have to have to someone in order to receive health benefits, I'd prefer their specified relationships be expansive, but I would rather everyone have full access to healthcare. As long as borders exist, I would prefer that immigration restrictions recognize a variety of relationships and families, but I would strongly prefer no borders at all. As long as we are locking people in prisons, I would prefer that incarcerated people can receive private visits from anyone they hold dear, but I'd rather see every prison wall fall.

Coupledom Doesn't Benefit Everyone Equally

The rights and protections conferred by marriage and coupledom are also, effectively, theoretical. In practice, they can be and are frequently denied. People who are Black, Indigenous, racialized, disabled, poor, and/or use stigmatized drugs are regularly denied protection and dignity in medical, legal, and bureaucratic settings, whether they're single, partnered, or married. There is no point in talking about laws and policies without looking at how they play out in people's real lives. In the anthology *That's Revolting: Queer Strategies for Resisting Assimilation*, scholar Marlon M. Bailey points out,

> We should not assume, in a racist, sexist, heterosexist, and homophobic society, that all people will have access to the so-called rights and privileges that marriage purports to offer. Black people, especially Black queers, have never been able to rely on the state to see us as equal citizens entitled to the rights and privileges granted to our white counterparts. For many Black people, marriage has never been the answer to these problems simply because Black people's social institutions are not seen as worth honoring. We are locked out of these so-called protections even when we adhere to the social strictures that are supposed to enable such protections.[9]

As Bailey describes, marriage and coupledom are not a reliable path toward being able to access things like safe, dignified healthcare. Instead of trying to cram queer relationships into the category of "romantic relationships that confer legitimacy and deservingness," it would be great if we could just treat everyone with dignity and care.

Marriage can also be detrimental to poor and disabled people who receive state support money. In Ontario two people living together as "spouses," whether legally married or not, receive less money from Ontario Works (welfare) and the Ontario Disability Support Program than two single people would. The government of Ontario decides that you are spouses based on asking you questions like "Do friends and family members think you are a couple?" and "Do schools, doctors, or other organizations know you as a couple?"[10] This is not a beautiful expansion of the definition of partnership; this is the state ghoulishly reserving for itself the ability to dictate whether you get maybe barely enough to live on or absolutely not enough to live on. In the essay "Your Sex Is Not Radical," Yasmin Nair asks that we "demand that the state not determine whether we live or die based on what kinds of families or kinship groups we inhabit."[11] I agree: I'd much rather the benefits conferred on some people by marriage be liberated for the use of all.

I doubt that many people whose primary relationships are romantic or familial are explicitly thinking, "I'd like to focus more on my friendships, but the financial and legal benefits of setting my life up in a more socially normative way are just too good to pass up!" For the most part we just absorb our sense of values and priorities from among the options presented to us. And insurance systems didn't just spring fully formed from the earth; they were made by people as a reflection of our values and norms. However, they play a role in continuously reinforcing the dominance of the romantic couple and the nuclear family as the primary locus of care in people's lives.

If you want to move friendship closer to the centre of your life and materially support and care for your friends in a way that has more in common with what's expected of romantic and familial relationships, you will face very real obstacles to doing so. The possibility of diverting more time, effort, and resources to your friendships is constrained by the expectations and values within your own heart but absolutely also by material, external factors.

What Else Is Out There Beyond Coupledom?

In her essay "The Loves of Others," Hannah Black describes the couple form as "the most reductive, exclusionary and precarious imaginable method of meeting the probably universal need to feel close to and recognized by others."[12] In Black's experience, even though she considered coupledom as "an unforgivable privatization of love," it was hard to find satisfying alternatives. "Despite the efforts of radical groups and the bravery of marginalized communities, it mostly remains the case that in turning away from couple-form love, we are turning toward nothing. The hope or mirage of kindness among strangers, of love among friends, is at war with the intensive familiarity of romantic love." Abolition of an oppressive system always needs to go hand in hand with building something better, developing new skills, and giving more of our energy and resources and attention to alternatives.

In a conversation with my friend River about friendship, they observed, "When you're talking about wanting to get away from received romantic constructs and being able to be in chosen relationship with a variety of people, where everyone gets their needs met, you can only have that kind of freedom in a social safety net." We rely on romantic partners and families to meet a lot of our needs: both our emotional needs for companionship and affection and our more material needs for care. We will all at some point need a ride to the hospital or help with bathing, using the toilet, getting groceries, or preparing food. There is an expectation that it's romantic partners or family members who will step up to provide this care. If you want to, or have to, organize your life outside of the templates of the couple and the family, there is a very real risk of falling through the cracks unless there is a net to catch you.

I talk more about social safety nets in the next chapter, and, throughout the rest of the book, I talk about ways we can weave our social fabric tighter so that fewer people are left behind. However, as we work toward changing our social infrastructure on a broader scale, we can chip away in our own life at the overdependence on the family and couple forms. We can expand our circle of care, the people (and more-than-human beings) we feel responsibility for, outwards.

In his 2006 essay "For Lovers and Fighters," Dean Spade wrote about the concept of "treating your friends more like your lovers, and treating your lovers more like your friends." Treating your romantic partners more like your friends could involve trying "to be respectful and thoughtful and have boundaries and reasonable expectations." Treating your friends more like your lovers could look like making an effort to show your friends "special attention, honor ... [your] commitments to them, be consistent, and invest deeply in ... [your] futures together."[13]

Since I first read this it's been one of the foundational values by which I try to organize my relationships. And I'm not alone in moving friendship closer to the centre of my life and wanting to devote more of my resources to it: a therapist friend told me she's noticed more of her clients in the past few years seeking out "couples therapy" for their friendships. It is heartening to me to hear that people are increasingly interested in taking their friendships seriously in a way that had usually been reserved for romantic and familial relationships, putting money and time and effort into making them work.

One concrete way that you can centre your friendships is by increasing the range and intimacy of activities you share with your friends. Similar to Elizabeth Brake's "unbundling" of the legal rights usually bundled up in the institution of marriage, you can unbundle aspects of coupled life from the couple form. Anything you think of as being reserved for a romantic or familial relationship, you can also do within a friendship if you want to. It can be intimidating to start thinking "OK, what even *are* the types of things people do in a relationship?" I really like the "Relationship Anarchy Smörgåsbord" model for thinking through this.[14]

The Relationship Anarchy Smörgåsbord lays out a buffet of potential relationship components for people to pick and choose what they'd like to share. The idea is to proactively create a customized relationship rather than necessarily adopting a pre-bundled set of expectations, like "we're dating, so that means we have to have sex with each other, not have sex with anyone else, work toward marriage and cohabitation, and be each other's primary caregiver when the need arises." The "platters" you can help yourself to each contain multiple items. The Caregiving platter includes emergencies and end-of-life/death care. Physical Intimacy includes dancing, kissing, and co-sleeping. Under Time Spent Together, you can make decisions about how to handle holidays, birthdays, and dates. Other categories include Public Displays of Affection, Future Plans, and Financial.

It's a worthwhile exercise to try and inventory as many of your interpersonal needs as you can (someone to tell about your day, sex, nonsexual physical intimacy, someone to share meals with, be an emergency contact, etc.) and list the people in your life. See with whom you're currently doing what and who might be open to expanding your relationship to include other activities and aspects. Looking at the Smörgåsbord diagram helps me start thinking about who in my life I most enjoy sharing different activities with, whether it's cuddling or organizing big projects or doing arts and crafts. This exercise can also help you recognize unmet needs and desires in your life and start thinking about whether there are people you already know who might be able to meet them or whether you might want to seek out new relationships. I am always trying to expand my circle of care and to have more people in my life with whom I share mutual responsibility. This is both because it's fun and pleasant to share life with people and because I recognize the depths to which social safety nets have been shredded. All we have is each other.

SIX

Shredded Social Safety Nets

> Solidarity is the essential human process of recognizing that other people are real and their experiences matter. It is based in learning to evaluate the state of the world by the collective and not only by our own, individual experience. Solidarity is the action behind the revelation that each of us, individually, are not the only people with dreams.
>
> —SARAH SCHULMAN, *The Fantasy and Necessity of Solidarity*[1]

I know this probably isn't what you expected when you picked up a book about friendship, but understanding more about neoliberalism has helped me so much in understanding many of the struggles I've faced in my friendships. Neoliberalism is one of those terms that's used to describe such a wide swath of phenomena that people sometimes argue that it's meaningless. But I find it vital for describing some of the ideologies that shape our lives and that underlie so many things that pointing them out can feel like pointing at everything, like a fish trying to describe water.

The most general definition of neoliberalism is something along the lines of extending the range of things we think of in terms of the market — things that can be bought, sold, and valued in dollars — to encompass basically everything. It's epitomized by Margaret Thatcher's statement a 1987 interview that there is "no such thing" as society:

> I think we have gone through a period when too many children and people have been given to understand "I have a problem, it is the Government's job to cope with it!" or "I have a problem, I will go and get a grant to cope with it!" "I am homeless, the Government must house me!" and so they are casting their problems on society and who is society? There is no such thing! There are individual men and women and there are families and no government can do anything except through people and people look to themselves first.[2]

Bravely coming out against the existence of any collective responsibility to ensure children have homes, Thatcher emblematized neoliberalism's divestment from all forms of collectivity and its withdrawal into seeing only individuals — and families, but construed in the narrowest sense, leaving out extended families, chosen families, and every other care and kinship arrangement outside of the fortress of the nuclear family. Under neoliberalism, institutions formerly thought of as essential parts of the public good, like hospitals, housing, and the postal service, are expected to turn a profit. American historian Gary Gerstle calls neoliberalism "a creed that calls explicitly for unleashing capitalism's power."[3]

The Unravelling of Human Life

Neoliberalism is defined as much by what it destroys as by what it creates, and it's perhaps easiest to see its traces via the aspects of human life it's ground into dust for profit. In order to convert every aspect of life into a product, neoliberalism needs to undermine and unravel institutions that provide people with care. Institutions that are crushed or starved under neoliberalism include labour unions, community organizations, and government programs that support things like affordable housing, education, and healthcare. A neoliberal regime must also suppress resistance to this social unravelling, which it often does by investing generously in surveillance and policing, even as other programs are cut. On every level, a neoliberal way of life severs bonds and encourages us to think of ourselves as fundamentally distinct from one another, as opposed to entwined and interdependent.

In his book *Caring for Souls in a Neoliberal Age*, theologian Bruce Rogers-Vaughn argues that "neoliberalism has become so encompassing and powerful that it is now the most significant factor in shaping how, why, and to what degree human beings suffer."[4] He writes that he started noticing a collection of new and consistent attributes among people who came to him for pastoral counselling, including "a marked increase in self-blame … as well as an amorphous but potent dread that they are somehow teetering on the edge of a precipice."[5] People were quick to locate the source of their malaise within their own personal trauma history. Even when they identified that they were experiencing racism, homophobia, misogyny, or any combination of those, they were still inclined to believe that "only they could do anything about their problems."[6] Rogers-Vaughn describes this orientation toward the world, and the difficulties of living in it, as the imprint of a neoliberal society that is "based on the principles of individualism and competition."[7]

Political theorist Wendy Brown describes what happens when everyone becomes, first and foremost, an entrepreneur: "We have no guarantee of security, protection, or even survival ... [and are] at persistent risk of failure, redundancy, and abandonment."[8] In her book *The Social Safety Net*, Nora Loreto writes, "It's impossible to fully isolate individuals from one another, but through things like debt, low wages, and increasing responsibilities (that members of the community might have helped with before), we each suddenly realize that maybe we really are alone in this world."[9] These structural factors — debt, low wages, and increasing responsibilities — make it harder for us to care for one another. And worse, the ideology of neoliberalism, which has suffused our flesh like microplastics, has made us wonder if we even should care for one another. "You don't owe anyone anything" is a neoliberal belief you might hear coming from the mouths of both devoted capitalists and nominally progressive therapy influencers. Anyone who is telling you to protect your own peace and contentment over the impositions of others is coming at you with a fundamentally Margaret-Thatcher-ass take.

If there's a central argument to this book, it's the admittedly not groundbreaking idea that friendship is hard because everything else is hard. And neoliberalism is at the centre of why things are so hard. Material conditions matter a lot, regardless of our ideals. The presence or absence of a social safety net, the cost, stability, and quality of the homes we live in, the wages we earn and how they compare to the costs we are expected to bear, what recourse and supports we have when things go sideways — these things profoundly shape our lives. They determine the amount of "free time" (which is itself a creepily neoliberal term) we have and whether we're squeaking by on the bare minimum or have plenty to share. The material conditions of our lives have a big impact on our practical ability to care for one another. We're trying to pick up the slack in our friendships from decades of austerity and disinvestment, and friendship cannot carry that weight.

Even worse is what neoliberalism has done to our hearts. It has changed our very sense of what we are and how we fit in the world. It has not just been made harder to care for our friends; it's made us believe we don't have to. If you're sad, you should go to therapy, not demand emotional labour from your friends. If you're moving, you should hire movers, not ask people to help you carry your stuff. If you have an early-morning flight, you should just take a cab, not ask a friend for a drive. As a result, those of us who wish to be better friends, neighbours, and community members, who wish to weave ourselves more tightly into the social fabric, have not only material and logistical hurdles to overcome but also need to kill the Margaret Thatcher in our hearts and figure out how to acknowledge, celebrate, and tend to our interdependence.

Neoliberalization operates on a global scale. I came into political consciousness in the mid to late 1990s, the pre-9/11 political era in which I experienced the most salient political rallying point on the left to be opposition to globalization in general and the passage of NAFTA in particular. This was admittedly tough for even the most earnest middle schooler (me) to grasp. However, I feel grateful for having been introduced to the concept at a young age (folks, it's never too early to start teaching your kids about globalization) because it's something so insidious and pervasive that it's difficult to see. This also has a lot to do with people like me who are white and living in the Global North being strongly discouraged from thinking too hard about who is making our cheap clothes and taking care of our elders and why that is.

Starting in the 1980s, countries receiving aid through the World Bank and the International Monetary Fund (IMF) have been required to implement neoliberal policies like cutting healthcare and education funding, eliminating food subsidies, cutting wages, privatizing state-owned utilities like electricity and water, intensifying focus on resource extraction, and making it easier for foreign investors to profit from work done within the aid-receiving countries. The majority of countries in South America and Africa have received such loans, which they needed thanks to having been impoverished and immiserated by historical and ongoing colonization. Even the IMF's own research finds that neoliberal policies have been "oversold" and that the "benefits in terms of increased growth seem fairly difficult to establish when looking at a broad group of countries,"[10] while "the costs in terms of increased inequality are prominent."[11]

This unimaginably vast destruction of lives and ways of living has forced many people to uproot themselves from the places where they had community ties, the vital and delightful support of friends and family, and a sense of meaning and belonging. In exchange for the hope of better wages and the ability to ameliorate some of the privation and suffering to which neoliberalization has subjected their loved ones, people have become economic migrants and are subjected to some of the worst and most isolating conditions, like as domestic workers. Oxfam found that "80% of the world's 67 million domestic workers are women — 90% don't have access to social security, and more than half have no limits on their weekly working hours."[12] With little control over when and how much you work, how can you find the time and energy to see your friends or to take part in the hobbies, community groups, political movements, or religious and cultural celebrations that would allow you to make and strengthen friendships?

The emphasis on resource extraction is also undoubtedly hastening the climate crisis, which is already an important factor in uprooting people from their homes and communities and will only become more so. The United Nations High Commissioner for Refugees estimated that "84% of refugees and asylum seekers originate from 15 highly climate-vulnerable countries"[13] The report also notes that "a significant percentage of forcibly displaced and stateless people are living in the most climate-vulnerable environments in the world." Displaced from one unstable region to another and cut loose from their existing networks of care and resources, how are people supposed to build strong and lasting ties of friendship and community?

When we talk about why friendship is hard, we can't ignore people who are forced from their homes and communities due to economic collapse, state violence, climate-change-induced catastrophe, and other consequences of neoliberalism as the apotheosis of the centuries-long project of colonial capitalism. What could be less conducive to friendship than having to leave the place where you already know people, speak the language fluently, and know where to meet and hang out with people with similar interests and values, and starting over somewhere you might not have any existing ties and where you are much more likely to be subject to harsh and isolating working conditions?

What If People Were Just Allowed to Live?

People should be allowed to live: nobody should be deprived of a safe stable home, nourishing food, medical care, and the supports they need to live a life of their choosing. None of these things should be allocated based on people's ability to work or exploit the work of others, or on their personal friendships or likeability. We do not currently live in that world! And insofar as we don't, friendship is much harder. I think friendship would be easier in the presence of a social safety net: some kind of way of ensuring that everyone has access to the conditions necessary for flourishing.

As much as I love friendship, it should not be a factor in determining to what extent someone is able to get their basic needs met and be allowed to live. Leah Lakshmi Piepzna-Samarasinha writes wonderfully about this in their book *Care Work: Dreaming Disability Justice*. They describe the care collective that Loree Erickson, a "white Southern disabled queer femme anarchist," has organized and sustained for herself for the past 15 years to help her with dressing, bathing, and transferring, as well "the admin work of emailing, scheduling, and training potential care shifters."[14] Piepzna-Samarasinha is clear that Erickson's arrangement is "a deep possibility model, not a one-size-fits-all solution for everyone who needs care," and not something anyone can easily replicate because it "relies on her having access to a broad network of friends and acquaintances, a social and activist life where people know her and are interested in helping her out, something many people, especially sick, disabled, and mad people, are too socially isolated to be able to access."[15] We need ways of getting people's needs met at scale that are not predicated on anyone's popularity or likeability. The worst, meanest, most annoying person still deserves to eat, as much as charming and well-connected people do. When social care structures are absent, inadequate, or exclude people, we try to pick up the slack within individual relationships, and individual relationships aren't built for that. For our friendships to flourish, we need institutions and organizations dedicated to making sure people's needs are met, and we don't have those.

One of the institutions that can deliver care at scale is the state, through collecting taxes and providing funding for things like hospitals, schools, daycares, and non-market housing, and administering cash transfers via income assistance, disability benefits, and old-age pensions. When you think of a social safety net, it is likely that you think of a state. But it's worth mentioning that non-state networks of care existed long before the state, and for as long as there have been state social safety nets, there have been people excluded from them: non-citizens, Indigenous people, racialized people, queers, Mad, sick and disabled people, people who use stigmatized drugs, and so on.

Government social safety nets exclude people by design, not by accident. Nora Loreto both describes how Canada's social safety net was gutted by neoliberalism and also emphasizes that it was only originally established to bolster the well-being of English and French colonists as they carried out the genocide of Indigenous Peoples on this land.[16] You can't talk about education in Canada without talking about residential schools or about healthcare without talking about Indigenous people being denied care and non-consensually sterilized. Loreto's writing is an important reminder that there was no innocent, neutral, utopian version of the government social safety net prior to neoliberalism to which we can or should want to return. It's always been rotten.

Insofar as state social safety nets exist, I want them to move toward equity. But we also need to keep in mind that care at scale existed before the state as we know it. People excluded from state social safety nets have always organized other ways to care for each other. We will still be caring for each other after the state. Religious groups and institutions have been both the architects of some of the worst atrocities in the name of care, like Canada's residential school system, and also the means by which many people have accessed emergency or ongoing help with their physical and emotional needs. In the early 20th-century United States, fraternal organizations were the means by which many working-class people accessed services like medical care. There were organizations specifically for and by women, over 200 Black mutual aid societies in New Orleans alone,[17] and across the US southwest, *mutualistas* provided "cultural activities, education, healthcare, insurance coverage, legal protection and advocacy before police and immigration authorities, and anti-defamation activities" for Mexican immigrants in the late 19th century.[18] Unions have hired doctors, provided health insurance, and set up prepaid plans at hospitals for injured workers, as well as organized social activities like meals, parties, dances, sports teams, and choirs and provided "third spaces," like union halls, where union members and their families could gather socially.[19] Care has been organized for the end of life and beyond. Burial societies like Jewish *chevra kadisha* ensure that people who have died, including those with no family and friends to bury them, are provided a dignified and culturally appropriate burial.[20]

Where state-provided social safety nets exclude or actively harm some people, or where they're hollowed-out and crumbling thanks to neoliberalism, these types of organizations can grow again. But while neoliberal governments have broken and sold off state social safety nets, they have simultaneously eroded our ability to function collectively or even see ourselves as a collectivity with responsibility to one another. We've become the individuals that Margaret Thatcher, may she rest in piss, saw us as: people who don't necessarily see ourselves as owing each other anything. Undoing this damage must take place at both an individual level, as we rewrite our narratives about what we owe each other, and also a collective level, as we rebuild networks of care and support.

Weaving Our Own Safety Nets

In the absence of a social safety net, friendship is harder. When people are struggling to get our own needs met, we have less energy and time available for friendship and aren't as well placed to be generous either practically or emotionally. We'll be struggling to meet each other's needs on a one-on-one basis, when this is better done at scale. I think that the coming years will be hard ones and that they will call upon our skills at both friendship and community in two ways. First, our current system is going to continue to crumble and become even more untenable. More and more people will fall into worse and worse situations. I think we will see more authoritarian governments, more climate catastrophe and displacement, and more people fleeing autocratic regimes, state violence, and social breakdown. And we are going to need to work together both in our small interpersonal networks and in larger ways to survive. Second, as the current order falls apart, we're going to be doing a lot of work to build new things. In this moment of collapse, it's worth thinking about the numerous forms that social safety nets have taken. None of the ways of organizing care at scale that I mentioned above are perfect or applicable to every situation. There'll never be any one thing that works: we need everything.

There are also skills we can develop within our friendships — building trust, aligning our actions with our values, repairing damaged relationships — that we can extend outwards to our larger communities. As we develop more infrastructure to meet each other's needs, our friendships will benefit. We will be put into connection with more and a greater variety of people, and we will, I hope and believe, be able to act less often from a place of scarcity and desperation.

SEVEN

Lonely, Expensive Homes

> House meetings are the glue that binds. It is the space where we decide, together, what we want our home to be. It's how we reach consensus on large topics … like how we need to pack the rocks around the heating element in the barrel sauna so we don't trip the breaker, or where the cattle exclusion fencing needs to go, or whose guests can stay in the loft which nights, or how we'll manage the dogs when someone is out of town, or what our protocol is for saving bacon grease, or who's going to rally the dump run for that given week, or who will be responsible for procuring chicken feed, or which of us are excited to harvest the neighbor's olives for the community crush this Sunday.
>
> —SKY FUSCO, describing communal living in "Against Solitude"[1]

Samuel R. Delany's *The Motion of Light in Water: Sex and Science Fiction Writing in the East Village* recollects his experiences growing up as a gay Black New Yorker, raised in Harlem in the 1940s and 50s and coming of age in the East Village while in an open marriage with the white writer Marilyn Hacker.[2] It's one of my favourite books, and one thing I love about it is how detailed a picture it paints of the bohemian life he and his friends and partners were able to have. It is, among other things, an amazing case study in what life can look like if you have cheap rent and a strong community of artists and weirdos. He writes, "In the summer of 1961 no one had yet named it the East Village: it was still the Lower East Side. It was the cheapest neighborhood in Manhattan. Rumors of three- and four-bedroom apartments to be had for thirty-five dollars a month ran through the bohemian population of the city."[3] This translates to about $350 in contemporary money. People who've lived in Montreal, where I live, for a while might still have a room in a shared apartment that costs $350 for each roommate. Can you imagine what your life would be like if your rent was $350 a month? Even for a room in a shared apartment? What if you could pay that much for a three- or four-bedroom apartment all to yourself with plenty of space to work on your art and spare rooms where you could invite friends to visit or take in anyone in your life who lost their housing?

It does sound from Delany's description that rent that cheap was the exception rather than the norm, something that would entice people to a neighbourhood they wouldn't necessarily choose otherwise. And they might have been pretty shitty apartments. But in the same book he also writes about becoming friends with the poet W.H. Auden and his partner Chester Kallman, who "told us they paid, I believe, $148 a month for their own St. Marks Place flat — which whispered to us of the luxurious life truly successful writers might lead."[4] This was likewise in the early 1960s, so would be about $1,480 today. Although Delany's characterization is a little tongue-in-cheek, that's close to what my roommate and I pay, and we do not lead a particularly luxurious life. Our apartment is spacious and lovely, but drafty and full of holes, and everything that can stop working frequently does. In 1961 minimum wage in New York was a dollar an hour, which $10 in today's money.[5] So, if you had a household of three or four people, each making minimum wage, and paying a total of $350 in rent, the household — not each person — would have to work a total of 35 hours a month to make rent. If there were three of you, you could each pay rent by working three hours a week.

The Beat generation poet Diane di Prima's *Recollections of My Life as a Woman: The New York Years* also recounts life in this era and scene. Describing her life as a single mother and artist in Manhattan, she is detailed and unsparing about the dangers and discomforts of being as broke as she was. She writes about moving in 1955 into a railroad apartment in Hell's Kitchen, a neighbourhood in midtown Manhattan. The toilet was shared with other tenants, and the apartment was heated only by a wood stove in its kitchen. The apartment had a living room, bedroom, kitchen, and a smaller room she called the "wood shed," which she used to store art supplies and firewood scrounged from the street. Her rent was $33, just under $400 in 2025 money, and she worked for pay 20 hours a month, mostly modelling for painters.[6] That cheap rent allowed her, a working-class artist, to live and work within an expansive community of artists; it was possible to be a working artist in Manhattan without astronomical commercial success or generational wealth.

We have bizarre horny sci-fi novels like *Dhalgren* and trenchant commentary on gentrification like *Times Square Red, Times Square Blue* because Delany had cheap rent and was able to live on the proceeds of some pretty weird (meant in the most affectionate way possible) books and spend lots of time reading, hanging out with other writers, and cruising. We have di Prima's gorgeous, unsparingly furious and loving feminist poetry because she was able to live, raise kids, and run Poets Press and the newspaper *The Floating Bear* in a dense metropolis full of opportunities to collaborate and share inspiration with the other poets, painters, actors, and weirdos she describes in her memoir.

I can only run *my* small press and write this book because I live in Montreal and am clinging by my fingernails to decently affordable rent that allows me to freelance part-time and do unprofitable art stuff the rest of the time. The more your rent costs, the more you have to work, obviously. If you only had to work half as much as you do now, what would you do with the rest of your time? Are there projects you've daydreamed about that you'd be able to devote time to realizing? And what would it mean for your friendships, your ability to show up for people in your life when they're in need, your capacity to spend time together in a leisurely unscheduled way, your interest in political organizing and community projects? My day job is in affordable housing, and pretty much every day of my life I feel vivid rage and grief about everything that would be possible if we weren't all scrabbling to pay our stupid rent.

Unaffordable Housing Ruins Your Life

There is a huge psychic burden to struggling to afford your home. Rent that is difficult to afford costs you not only the time you spend working for pay but also the time you spend thinking and worrying about housing. Most people I know spend a lot of time looking at apartment listings even if they're not immediately planning to move. We do so in a spirit of fretful research, wondering just how bad it would be if we did have to move. Expensive housing constrains what is possible for you and even your imagination of how things could be different. It increases the consequences of failure to a catastrophic level. If there were a fire, if you and your partner broke up, if you just wanted to experiment with living somewhere else, would it put your entire survival at risk?

The state of housing affordability makes it much harder to leave a living situation and sometimes by extension, a relationship, whether it is actively dangerous or just unsatisfying. It constrains the extent to which you even consider leaving. It raises the bar of what you are willing to tolerate. Maybe your relationship isn't great, but if you moved, you'd probably have to pay twice as much rent, so is it really worth leaving? It may seem contradictory to talk about investing deeply in relationships on one hand and about flexibility and ability to leave them on the other. But both are important: being stuck in an abusive relationship because you can't afford to move is not the same as investing deeply in a neighbourhood you love.

When I moved cities a few years ago, I'd already been thinking for years about the move. One of the main reasons I held on so long was because I had lived for years in a nice studio apartment in a building owned by a non-profit. Half of my neighbours paid subsidized rent, and the other half, myself included, paid rent that was not subsidized but that also didn't generate profit for anyone. It was a friendly building where people would stop and chat to each other and could ask their neighbours for help with things like moving a piece of furniture or pet-sitting.

When I first moved into that building, my rent was a good deal, although not astonishing. Over the years I lived there, average rental housing costs soared as my rent went up a modest 2% or so a year. By the time I left, if I had wanted to move into a similarly sized apartment, I could easily have paid twice as much for a worse home. I knew that if I moved out of the city I could probably never come back. What would you do if you knew that you could move out of your place and be able to find another affordable home when you came back? I prevaricated for years, struggling to fit myself into a city that had stopped feeling like home. I wish I had made the move sooner, but the state of housing affordability made the decision much less reversible than it could have been. The rational choice was to wait until the situation became untenable.

I think a lot about people who are in various kinds of terrible housing situations: mouldy walls, abusive partners, scary neighbours, or isolation from friends, community, resources and anything else that makes life liveable. The extent to which housing has become difficult to afford is an obvious danger to people's lives: consider the disabled people in Canada applying for medical assistance in dying solely because they don't have a safe or affordable home.[7] I also think a lot about the opportunities for joy, connection, creative work, and adventure that we miss out on because of how tightly we have to cling to whatever semi-OK housing situation we're in.

Legalize Roommates!

Like I mentioned above, I've worked in affordable housing for a long time, so I have no shortage of ideas on how we could unfuck housing on a large scale: stop treating it like an investment, stop subsidizing the construction and ownership of single-family detached homes and treating them as something we should all aspire to, make building multi-unit buildings easier, and invest on a vast scale in non-market housing. While none of these are things we can bring about on our own, there are choices we can make as individuals to live in ways that are more conducive to friendship, art, free time, and the other things that make life worthwhile.

When I moved back to Montreal in 2022 after two years of pandemic solitude in Ottawa, I knew I wanted — needed — not to live alone anymore. I answered an ad on the Facebook group Chez Queer seeking "a mature person (no age limit) who also appreciates direct communication, who is community minded, likes spending time in common spaces, is interested in being a part of a home with distribution of responsibilities and ownership, is emotionally aware, likes animals/would benefit from animal companionship." Two years later my roommate gave me a pair of house-shaped beaded earrings to celebrate our roommate anniversary.

One of the reasons I moved back to Montreal is that it feels less dogmatic about ways that people's lives should look at any given age: I love how I often see old weirdos around the city, people decades older than me who are still putting on elaborate outfits to walk their dogs and are still deeply engaged in organizing and art and life. I feel like here I can see a path to grow older while still being true to my values and desires. And that includes being a renter and living with roommates as someone who's approaching 40, something that's unremarkable among the people I spend time with here but would elicit concern, pity, or scorn elsewhere.

Apartments here were mostly built for large Catholic families, so they tend to be large and easy to reconfigure as households change. When I interviewed my friend Julia, another Montrealer, about ways she shows care for people in her life, one of the things she mentioned was that she has made it a priority to have a spare room friends can borrow: "It's been important for close and less-close friends as a space during breakups, during visits to town, and during other kinds of life transitions."

And yet, as I was writing this book, our building was sold. The same day I received my editor's notes on this book, my roommate and I got a letter in the mail notifying us that our home's new owners were evicting us. Montreal may be more roommate-friendly than many other places, but as the housing crisis here intensifies, that is changing. Big apartments are being divided into smaller ones to increase landlords' profits, and there is immense competition for apartments that a normal person can afford, whether on the private market or in non-market housing. My roommate and I want to keep living together, so we're applying for housing co-ops, and it has been an ongoing conversation whether we should just allow co-op selection committees to assume that we're a couple, since being roommates might harm our chances of being selected. Montreal may become less of a roommate paradise and more like other cities.

Many US municipalities even have bans against more than two unrelated people living together in a household. A 2022 study from the American Enterprise Institute found that "zoning codes in 23 of the 30 largest U.S. cities or nearby suburbs, impose limits on occupants deemed 'unrelated' [by blood, adoption, or marriage]."[8] Even right-wing think-tanks find that goofy. Anti-roommate provisions seem to be less common in in Canada but not unheard of.[9] For example, tenants in rent-geared-to-income (subsidized) housing in Ontario face more restrictions on their household composition than their neighbours who pay market rents.[10] Like every law, roommate bans are enforced in an unequal way that arbitrarily targets and criminalizes poor and racialized people. Writing in *The Atlantic*, Michael Waters found that many US cities that banned roommates enforced those bans almost solely against Latinx households.[11]

Roommate bans enforce, in the most literal sense, who we are allowed to care about and share intimate aspects of our life with. They impose a financial penalty on being single or not wanting to live with a romantic partner or nuclear family. But I would like to humbly recommend living with roommates if you can. Not only is it cheaper — even in relatively affordable Montreal I'd be hard-pressed to find an apartment I could afford on my own — but it's also one of the best things about my life. Not all roommate households are as close as mine — we spend lots of time talking about things from current events to the latest gossip to unsnarling complicated issues with our dates or families of origin, we help each other out, we loan each other money, we share a lot of food and supplies — but I believe there is still a lot to be said for sharing day-to-day life with someone who is not a relative or romantic partner. My roommate and I each have our own friends, dates and families, but they've come to overlap more and more in the time we've lived together, as we've come to know each other's people and build our own friendships with them. I haven't dated anyone seriously in the three years we've lived together, but I've still been able to benefit from having a "default person" I see every day. We generally know what's going on with each other, can provide each other with day-to-day help and care, and can talk through things that are going on in our lives:

> "I just got a weird text, what do you think this means?"
> "I saw a poster for a protest I'm thinking of going to if you're interested."
> "Do you need anything from the store?"

I find so much benefit in having the person I share my everyday life and responsibilities with not be a romantic partner or family member. Separating out the day-to-day care of cohabitation from the higher-intensity care of intimate romantic or familial relationships makes more sense to me. It takes down the temperature, separating out my worth and loveability as a person from whether or not I've done my dishes that day. Although, New York City's rent-stabilization laws define a family member of the main tenant as any person "who can prove emotional and financial commitment, and interdependence" with them, so maybe we are family after all.[12]

Big Friendly Households

In writing this chapter, I sought out people who have lived in much larger households than I have to see how it has shaped their lives. When I interviewed Willy, who spent 11 years living in a 20-person house in San Luis Obispo, they mentioned how different it was to go through breakups while living in a large household versus while living alone:

> [If you live alone] you can reach out to people on the phone, you can make plans to meet up. But the immediacy of having your support network close to you as a coping mechanism, and to remind you about the people who care for you and support you is so huge. I was never in an abusive relationship or anything, but I think about the inclination to return to unhealthy relationships as something that happens out of a desperation [that comes from] the way we live. When you live in an apartment alone [while going through a breakup], you're completely alone, and you're constantly reminded of how nice it was to have somebody around.

Willy always had people around and whether or not they were in a romantic relationship at any given time, they always had support, company, and people to share the daily highs and lows of life.

That said, making your household a more communal one will be annoying and inconvenient. The more people you let into your life and the more you depend on each other, the more annoying and inconvenient it will be. Things will never be just as you envisioned them or just as you left them when you went out this morning. But they might be better: someone might have baked cookies or invited a person over who you're about to hit it off with. "Convenience kills," Willy put it, reflecting that "it's like driving your car versus riding a bike: yeah, you have to put in more effort, but you know how numb you feel after you drive your car every day, over and over? Adding some friction [to your life] can be so good for you."

Lisa Sibbett writes a newsletter called *The Auntie Bulletin* about how and why to have kids in your life when you aren't a parent. In her essay "The Radical Politics of Auntiehood," she recommends extending your circle of care outwards; she describes the nuclear family model as expecting "each household to fend for themselves."[13] In contrast, people who have a large circle of people they see regularly and relate to as kin "may know what's needed simply by virtue of being around one another," so it's "easy to leap into action and provide support when we know what's happening in each other's lives." This is not just nicer and more convivial. When we share resources, we can buy less, which means we can work less, which means we have more time to continue deepening our relationships with one another.

Things are wildly expensive right now. It is increasingly unfeasible to have a whole house, a whole car. Many of us outsource, privatize, and use apps to order gig workers around to do things we would otherwise have had to organize with people we know. If we don't like a gig worker, we can destroy their livelihood by leaving them a less-than-glowing review, without having to interact with them as people. Any amount we can divest ourselves from this fake "sharing" into actual relationships is bound to be good for our hearts, even if it is inconvenient — especially if it is inconvenient.

Kate, another person I spoke to who has lived for many years in various kinds of communal housing, reflected,

> Having a community of people I knew I could come back to [at home] made me braver in going out and pursuing the friendships I wanted. I realized I love planning events and hosting things. It's a terrible feeling when you want to plan something and you realize, *I only have three people to invite to this*, and start to think, *I must not be social. I must not be a cool person.* But when I had a community of people [already] around me [at home], I could involve them and start inviting people, and it gave me the confidence to do that and start bringing people together. If you have community, it's so much easier to keep building that community because I don't feel like I'm starved for social connection.

Kate's household leans into community not only in smaller gatherings but also by hosting two big house parties a year. One roommate, a dancer, choreographs a special four-move dance for each party and teaches it to everyone who attends "because we've found people will dance if they know what to do." Each party has a theme, ranging from "masquerodeo [masquerade + rodeo]" to "under the sea," with special surprises for guests: for the "under the sea party," one roommate filled a broom closet with test tubes of bioluminescent algae.

The siren song of living alone is deeply compelling, and I'm not holding a gun to your head about it. There are a lot of ways to live a life in deep connection with others, and they don't necessarily have to be right there inside your house. But I think there's a lot to be said for living as cheaply and sociably as you can, and as Kate points out, having a sociable home situation can drastically lower barriers to building connections outside of your home. When you live with people who aren't your family or romantic partner, less of your day-to-day care and social needs will fall on your family or partner, if you have one, freeing up that relationship to take whatever shape is most conducive. And the cheaper your housing is, the more flexible your life is and the more you're able to align the way you spend your time with your values.

EIGHT

Work, the Joy-Eater

> I'm pretty sure that if you put all your energy into the things you believe in, it will pay off in the long run. You will become really good at what you love, gain a strong sense of self, have a community to fall back on. Unseen avenues will open and you will have real, solid, long term security.
>
> —CINDY CRABB, on why you should quit your job, live within your means, and do what you love in *Doris #15: DIY Anti-Depression Guide*[1]

The extent to which a lot of people's lives would need to change a lot to prioritize friendship became clear to me after I started working freelance. Freelancing was never something I had expected or aspired to do — it always sounded too hard. I ended up doing it because I had to abruptly quit a truly awful job, and then I got an extremely cool job that was 10 hours a week and had to fill in the gap. Before that I'd spent the previous decade working desk jobs, first in offices and then, after the spring of 2020, from home. It would take a lot to get me to ever work in an office again.

Two months after I started freelancing, I went on a three-week road trip across the continent with a friend who was driving out and offered to let me tag along. We ate a lot of candy, listened to a lot of music, had a lot of long meandering conversations, and developed a lot of inside jokes. I worked a few hours here and there, and a bunch before and after, but it was mostly just summer fun, and I was and am so grateful to have had the flexibility to take off for a few weeks.

Three months after that, the same friend underwent an intense surgery in another city. As I described in the introduction to Part 2, I made plans to be there for the week of their surgery, but when it turned out they needed another pair of hands for more of their recovery, I ended up staying for about six weeks and then returning on and off throughout the following few months. That first month I woke up early every day and did a few hours of paid work before going to the hospital. I answered work emails on my phone while my friend was sleeping or undergoing a procedure outside of their room. I did more work back on whatever friend's couch I sleeping on that week while stuffing my face with takeout after another day of forgetting to eat. It was by no means a time of ease and rest; as you can imagine, it kind of kicked my ass to keep all those balls in the air and keep making money.

But if I'd still been at one of my office jobs, I wouldn't have been able to do it at all. I wouldn't have been able to do my work at odd hours or to ramp it up and down at will. I wouldn't have been able to take a paid leave of absence from work and maybe not even an unpaid one. Because the person I was caring for wasn't a spouse or family member, it wasn't necessarily a relationship that straight people, and institutions and policies created by straight people, would recognize as important. Few people in my life have jobs that allow them to take paid time off to care for their partners or families. But even those who do probably can't do it for their friends or for their dates and lovers outside of a relationship that looks like a straight person's.

That friendship didn't survive the following year, as it happens. But even if I had to do it all over knowing that, I would make the same choices. It was one of the most meaningful periods in my recent life and a crucible in which my values were tested and clarified. I feel strongly that when someone you love is sick or dying you should be able to make caring for them a priority if you want it to be one. Conversely and additionally, when someone is sick or dying, they should be able to access any type of care they want or need, regardless of who, if anyone, loves them. But it's only been within the past two years of my life, since I started freelancing that I have been able to do put my values into practice. I would have always identified friendship as being one of my core values and priorities, if not first among them. But in terms of how I spent my time, when push came to shove, I prioritized work. I don't think it was wrong to do so, from an ethical or a practical standpoint. I had rent to pay.

I still work too much. People close to me (lovingly) make fun of me about the disjunction between my stated belief that work is bad and to be minimized, and the length of time I nevertheless spend hunched over my laptop and the contracts I continue to take on despite complaining about being overwhelmed. But when I shifted work a little further from the centre of my life, I realized that no matter what I feel in my heart that my values are, my actual values emerge from the way I live my life and how I choose to spend my time, energy, money, and other resources. I would tell you that I value community and that true security emerges from networks of care, but my behaviour was a constant desperate scrabble to accumulate money and stability.

In his 2010 essay "It's So Queer to Give Away Money," Dean Spade writes,

> In a culture with a decreasing safety net, there is enormous fear-based pressure to save for retirement, unemployment, disability, children, and other life changes. A system that individualizes risk encourages people to look out for themselves alone and steel themselves against harm, knowing that they may face vulnerability alone. What kinds of structures would our communities need to put in place together so that we could trust that we would be cared for and that hoarding does not make the world safer for us? How can our queer and trans histories with caring for loved ones with AIDS, supporting youth abandoned by their families, and supporting queer and trans elders offer models?[2]

I don't know the answer to the rhetorical questions that Spade poses. I don't live in a world where we can all trust that we will receive care when we need it, regardless of social popularity or access to wealth. One of my favourite works of speculative fiction, *Everything for Everyone: An Oral History of the New York Commune, 2052–2072*, by Eman Abdelhadi and M.E. O'Brien, compellingly imagines such a world.[3] I also owe a debt to *The*

Dawn of Everything: A New History of Humanity by David Graeber and David Wengrow, which looks at the range in ways societies have been organized over the existence of human life, demonstrating what Graeber elsewhere calls "the ultimate, hidden truth of the world," which is that the world "is something that we make, and could just as easily make differently."[4] But like everything I'm writing about here, there are ways we can shift our mindsets, habits, and relationships within the current system. Making such changes within our own lives will develop our capacity to work toward larger, systemic changes.

The first years of the ongoing COVID-19 pandemic radicalized many people with regards to the role of work in their lives. I have to state first that the most important change with regard to COVID and work is that a lot of people were murdered by being knowingly forced to labour in dangerous conditions. I will never forget the clarity of the tweet I saw, which reposted an article about the shortage of restaurant workers by pointing out that they were a group who had faced one of the highest rates of death from COVID, stating, "The workers you're looking for are in the ground."[5] We know too that these dead are disproportionately Black, brown, and Indigenous, as well as those with the fewest legal protections, such as immigrant, undocumented, and incarcerated workers. And a lot of other people have become too sick or disabled to work in the same way they had before. Since the first time I got COVID, I think much more slowly, forget more readily, take longer to find words. I was infected at a mandatory in-person work event where I was the only person to consistently wear a mask. I was too new in the job to feel like I could say no and also too new to have any sick leave. I will never forgive those bosses.

I had something close to the best-case work scenario in 2020: a secure, decently paying work-from-home desk job. Even so, it cranked up an existing sense of cognitive dissonance to an unignorable volume. Something deeply important and terrifying was happening and I was at my silly laptop writing silly blog posts and tweets. The work was hectic — we had to reconfigure an imminent in-person conference to take place online instead — but it was obviously not that important. Even though I had a relatively good work situation, it absolutely sucked shit and made it clear to me that to work through that moment like usual required some heavy-duty dissociation.

For those of us fortunate enough to survive the first few years of COVID, the term "pandemic epiphanies" became a commonplace, as two-thirds of workers in the US apparently "reconsidered the role of work in their lives."[6] I am personally very worried and curious about the remaining third who didn't. I worked straight through, but people in my life who were out of work and receiving emergency benefits had, sometimes for the first time in their adult lives, space to consider what they actually enjoyed and wanted from their lives. And the answer was often "less work, more life." Work was always standing between us and the things that mattered. As long as there have been jobs, people have worked them while their hearts have been elsewhere. But the beginning of the COVID pandemic brought this into sharper focus, coming as it did after decades of austerity.

Better Ways to Spend Our Time

In Chapter 7, I wrote about how expensive rent constrains our imagination. Housing costs and jobs are closely linked, of course. The more expensive your rent is the harder it is to leave a job. When it is hard to afford the necessities of life, you have very little slack. You have little ability to be without income for a while if you tell a bad job to go fuck itself. You will have to eat more shit because you have little choice, or feel yourself to have little choice. It is in the best interest of bosses and corporations for you to be squeezed almost to your breaking point. An employee who is in debt, with no financial cushion and already struggling to pay their rent, is less likely to quit, complain, or fight back when their boss commits wage theft, gives them a crappy schedule, or generally treats them as disposable. Employees in vulnerable and precarious situations are also easier to frighten away from collective action.

In *Lost in Work: Escaping Capitalism*, Amelia Horgan writes, "Because so much of our time is spent at work, our ability to find alternative sources of joy or meaning are reduced, … possible countervailing sources of recognition — from friendship, from our hobbies, from shared social practices — dissolve."[7] There's a vicious cycle here: work eats up a lot of the time and energy that would allow us to develop and sustain networks of care. If more of us had those networks of care, we wouldn't have to work so much: we'd be able to share and collaborate more. Instead of having to individually pay for products and services, we'd have relationships that would allow us to share resources (tools, art supplies, food) and tasks (childcare, home repairs, anything that needs or benefits from more than one set of hands).

Say I need to put up a shelf. If I work all the time, I'll probably just buy a power drill. If I don't work much, maybe I have plenty of time to sit on my stoop and chat to neighbours, and I know them well enough that I can ask to borrow their drill. Or I've got time to go across town and borrow one from a friend. Or there's lots of people in my city who also don't have to work all the time, and they run a tool library I can borrow one from. I can acquire the use of a drill either by trading a bunch of my time or using that time to build relationships. I talk more about this in Chapter 10.

I think it's worth being specific here about my work situation and class status to situate where I'm coming from. My family paid for my university, so I graduated with a bachelor's degree without debt. I spent most of my 20s working in kitchens, then became an office temp, and through that got into decent-paying office jobs. After about a decade of that I had a collection of skills and relationships that have allowed me to freelance. I freelance both because it allows me to live in a way that is more pleasant and better aligned with my values and because I was reaching the end of my ability to work 40 hours a week. I am pretty crazy; I also experience a lot of painful and debilitating physical consequences when I work full-time, and I think a lot more people do than we think. My mother dropped out of school in about sixth grade and was mostly not able to work for money until her death when I was nine, but my dad spent his whole career as a crown attorney (what is called a district attorney in the

US). I absolutely don't have the kind of family money that makes paid work optional, but I do have the kind where if stuff went sideways in my life someone could probably give me $10,000. Very few people in my life have this kind of situation, so I am aware that it's rare and fortunate.

A lot of my friends have work further from the centre of their lives not by choice but because they're unemployed or employed in precarious, informal, or criminalized ways, and often because they're disabled. If you don't work, unless you're independently wealthy (hello, where did you get this weird anarchist book), you probably, in lieu of work, are forced to spend endless amounts of time and effort navigating humiliating and cruel bureaucracies in exchange for meagre, barely liveable sums of money. This too is an injustice that draws us away from friendship and the living of life. Other people in my life have moved work further from the centre of their lives by working seasonally or working at jobs that are easier to quit and either come back to or find another one of. Others have deprioritized work by not trying as hard, by calling in sick, or by doing their creative work on the clock. As social safety nets have eroded, surveillance technologies have advanced and economic inequality has worsened, making these options less and less viable.

There are advantages to having a job where you have to be physically present but don't have much to do, but the office jobs I've had where I had a lot more time than work were soul-crushing. At one job, even as a young try-hard who always angled to be given more responsibilities and more projects, I still always had many empty hours. The problem was that this free time could only take place in a cubicle in front of a computer, so it inherently could only be filled with tasks that, if not work, were nevertheless work-shaped. I could read as many articles online as I wanted but I couldn't go for a walk or embroider or cook or talk to friends. I could message people but not see their faces.

Where Is Life?

My friend Meghan, who we'll hear more about in Chapter 12, came up in the male-dominated field of engineering wanting to advance in her career and be a manager and a role model. But as she put more energy and care into community preparedness and Indigenous solidarity work, she found that she was less emotionally invested in her career and that her workplace was pulling back its support from her as well:

> These people whose respect I wanted didn't want me to say the word "Palestine" out loud at work and no longer trusted me to manage people because I could "poison their minds." I'm dead in the water professionally, and what a great time to be dead in the water. I realized that life is not at work. Life is over there with your community preparedness thing and your Indigenous friends.

I really appreciated Meghan's framing of looking for where the "life" is rather than following your desires:

> My desires are not necessarily trustworthy in the ways that they are deeply formed under consumer neoliberal capitalism. So how do I find authenticity in my desires outside capitalism, white supremacy, etc, so that I can choose for myself consciously, without getting hung up in, *I can have everything I want and that's great.*

Your desires can be distorted by social pressures and expectations. But a sense of "where life is" is not so easily co-opted. We may desire power over others, security, and nice things, but it is harder to look at those and tell yourself, "that's where life is."

It is a self-protective impulse to understand the worst aspects of your life as immutable, to blunt some of your suffering by making yourself believe that it's inevitable. However, it is vital to, if nothing else, keep alive our capacity to imagine things being otherwise. The ability to imagine a better world than the one we currently inhabit is like a stove's pilot light: a little flame we keep alight that keeps alive the possibility of sparking a bigger flame and greater changes.

One of the feelings that surprised me when I was first coming out as trans was how painful and humiliating it felt to desire my life to be otherwise than it had been and to admit to wanting better. I was ashamed to realize how much suffering and numbing out I'd accepted as the natural order of things, and I was also ashamed to reach hopefully out for something more. Sometimes you just have to eat shit and there's no way around it, but sometimes you're eating shit and convincing yourself shit is the only type of food that's ever existed. Putting aside whether it's possible, I think it's vital to think what your life would look like with less work. Honestly, if you have always worked it might be too hard to imagine a life without working for pay, so you can start by imagining if you worked one day less a week, or half as many hours. What would you do with the time? What projects have you dreamed of but put off? And what would it mean for your friendships? What if you didn't feel that bone-deep exhaustion every night? If your work didn't completely wring you out so all you felt able to do in the evening was scroll on your phone in front of the TV? Admittedly I'm an extrovert and I always wish I had more time to see my friends, go to community events and meetings, travel, and work on weird little projects with people. That's where life is for me, and it doesn't have to be where life is for you. But the question is worth asking.

WHAT ARE SOME WAYS YOUR FRIENDS HAVE CARED FOR YOU?

This memory of good care happened at a time where I was really down and completely vulnerable to someone doing something for me. I didn't realize it, and my friends certainly didn't realize it. They'd invited me over for dinner before, but this felt different. They did *everything* for me. Plied me with nice drinks, fed me appetizers, asked questions about my day while the two of them fluttered about the kitchen in a joyous fashion. And that's an important point too; they didn't have to *mask the burden*, they truly enjoyed cooking food and serving it to me. They didn't even realize I was so vulnerable; this is just how they do things. As the light dimmed outside, we set a gorgeous table and lit candles. There was a charcuterie board and wine and lo and behold, French onion soup with so many melty cheeses on top. It wasn't something out of the ordinary, but it was what I really needed right then, for someone to just take care of me for an hour and put great food in me. The effortlessness of their ongoing and gentle care warms me up even to reflect upon, and it's something I aspire to implementing in my life.

—KAT

One thing that comes to mind is spending nights at my best friend's small apartment. Going home together from events, talking about everything and everyone, spending the morning lying around and going on a walk. I think I have a toothbrush at her place. I guess it's the act of sharing her personal space and trusting me with it. We also often stay at her grandmother's place outside of our hometown. Sharing such a familial space is also a level of trust that makes me feel very cared for.

—ERIN

I think there's something so powerful about being cared for when you're sick. About someone feeding you the right meal or hot drink to comfort you when you're low. About someone tucking you into bed. It's happened in lots of little and big ways over the years. I grew up with a network of family friends, with a bunch of faux and real siblings, and I think the communalism of that really rubbed off on me. The knowing that there is someone with the resources to help you with your problem, somewhere in your community. I've also been very moved by packages and letters and messages, by gifts and texts and hangouts. I don't know how to pin this down, it turns out. It all accretes to so much more and evaporates when I try to talk about it.

—JULIA

I mentioned in passing to a close friend that when I was a kid, I would collect dandelion heads; I thought if I concentrated all the wishes, maybe they'd really come true. Of course, on some level I know that wouldn't happen, but the magic of it, the hope, was enough to keep me doing it. My friend remembered this and, without telling me, learned to make watercolor pigment. He gathered dandelions and made paint from them and gave it to me as a surprise. Literal wishes to create art with. I don't think I've ever felt as seen and cared for as I did then. He paid attention; he saw some ancient, unfulfilled hope in me and, though it was not his responsibility, went out of his way to try to heal it, just because he could. Because I'm worth that. I don't think it'll ever leave me.

—CARA

PART THREE

TOWARD A FRIENDLIER WORLD

When I think about a life centred around a romantic partner versus a life dispersed amongst a large network of friends, sometimes I imagine the person primarily invested in their partner as being held up by one strong rope and the person who mainly has a lot of friendships being held aloft in a tangle of thin threads. The coupled person has someone in their life with a strong obligation to show up for them in a consistent, reliable way, but if they lose that one person, they're in big trouble. For the person who relies on a network of friends, one can drop out with little effect. But it is also easy for all those friends to allow their threads to fray or drop, assuming that theirs is just one among many.

Writing in *Yaari: An Anthology on Friendship by Women and Queer Folx*, Ameya Nagarajan describes her life as a "patchwork quilt" of relationships, as someone who "didn't have a partner, but I did have five or six very close friends I could call on, and I could be fairly sure one of them could be free at a pinch."[1] Conversely, Kurt Vonnegut wrote of married people whose social world narrows down to one another, "When a couple has an argument, they may think it's about money or power or sex, or how to raise the kids, or whatever. What they're really saying to each other, though, without realizing it, is this: You are not enough people!"[2] The disadvantage of the patchwork quilt is that any of these five or six close friends might not have felt a strong sense of obligation to Ameya, or even have known themselves to be a load-bearing part of her life. Vonnegut's married couple at least knows the other relies on them. As someone whose life is oriented primarily around bonds of friendship and has also been mostly romantically unpartnered for the past five years or so, I think a lot about the extent to which a network of friendships, supplemented with occasional Grindr hookups, is able to fill the role that a romantic relationship has played at other times in my life and can play for other people.

It's a nonmonogamous truism that expecting one person to fulfill way too many of your interpersonal needs is a recipe for failure. In a lot of straight relationships, it's also a recipe for burning out women. It just makes more sense to spread out your interpersonal needs among as many people as possible. But I do think there's a reason beyond convenience why people want to have a primary person with whom they've exchanged a commitment to try to be the main person to meet each other's needs. I think of that reason as "bottomlining." According to anarchist collective CrimethInc.'s guide to affinity groups, which I discuss more later, "bottomlining the supplying of a resource or the completion of a project" means "guaranteeing that it will be accomplished somehow, no matter what." For example, "if your group promises to provide the banners for an action, make sure they're ready, even if that means staying up all night the night before because the rest of your affinity group couldn't show up."[3] To me bottomlining is a lot of the appeal of having one central, committed relationship in your life: having a person who has a very strong expectation to be there for you. We can bring a greater sense of commitment and seriousness to our friendships by formally or informally pledging to bottomline an aspect of a friend's needs — to make sure that need is filled, whether we do it ourselves, call in someone else to help, pay for a service, or otherwise do our utmost to make sure it happens.

In this section of the book, I look at the way people are weaving the social fabric of their lives together more tightly, building outwards from their friendships to create networks that are greater than the sum of the individual relationships within them. I begin by talking about whiteness in Chapter 9, "Divesting from Whiteness," because for myself, the greatest barrier to genuine, reciprocal connection is my WASP heritage, and I can't talk about learning connection without talking about unlearning the lessons whiteness taught me.

In Chapter 10, "Investing in Shared Resources," I talk to people who are developing closer bonds with their communities by sharing skills, possessions, and space.

Chapter 11, "Organizing Together," shows how organizing and activism can be grounds for conviviality, joy, and friendship: the answer often involves food.

In Chapter 12, "Planning Together," I look at how planning for emergencies, whether natural disasters or interpersonal conflicts, is not only important but also a good way to deepen bonds of friendship and community.

Chapter 13, "Learning How (and Why) to Repair," looks at how making friends is fun, but repairing breaches in friendship is scary and hard; it can be tempting to just end a friendships. This chapter looks at some reasons why you might feel that way, and why it might be worth being brave and trying to mend a struggling relationship.

In Chapter 14, "Building Community and Friendship across Difference," I argue that intergenerational friendships and community relationships are a vital complement to friendships with people who are similar to you in age and stage of life. One of the best-established ways to form these, while certainly not the only one, is through religious practice.

Chapter 15, "Returning to Ritual, Celebration, and Grief," talks about how our friendships need containers where we can acknowledge and move through big feelings and important life changes: I make the case that it's worth finding ways to incorporate more ritual into our lives.

These are some of the essential components of assembling, extending, and maintaining a patchwork quilt of friendship. Regardless of whether you have or want familial or romantic relationships, warm, thoughtful, dedicated friendships and community ties improve every part of life.

NINE

Divesting from Whiteness

> It is this individual uncertainty on the part of white American men and women, this inability to renew themselves at the fountain of their own lives, that makes the discussion, let alone elucidation, of any conundrum — that is, any reality — so supremely difficult. The person who distrusts himself has no touchstone for reality — for this touchstone can be only oneself.
>
> —JAMES BALDWIN, "Letter from a Region in My Mind"[1]

Being a white person in a white supremacist world gives me a lot. Virtually wherever I go people will extend me greater benefit of the doubt than I deserve, and assume I am capable, intelligent, and worth knowing. Money and status will accrue more easily to me, and state and institutional violence is less likely to befall me. In many ways I will get more than I deserve, a surplus I believe I'll always be obligated to notice and redistribute.

It's Killing You Too

I also think white people in white supremacy have made an awful bargain. We get these benefits at the cost of our ability to be in reciprocal relationships of care, respect, and service with other people, other living things, and the lands we live in. I think that severing relationships is a core aspect of whiteness — not whiteness the skin colour but whiteness the system of domination and power that sorts people into different social locations, regardless of their values, politics, or desires.

Whiteness under white supremacist colonialist capitalism stands in the way of forming and maintaining bonds of friendship. I'm writing here from my own position and experience as a white person who is in conversation with racialized friends and writers. I am focusing here on whiteness not because I think that the harm white supremacy causes white people is the main or most important kind of harm it causes — it obviously isn't — but because it is what I can speak to.

Other theorists have tracked the intertwining of whiteness, white supremacy, colonialism, and capitalism, but they are bound so closely together that I speak about them together in this book. These are obviously huge topics, with hundreds of years of complex history binding them. As a white person, my desire is to shed some of the individualism I've learned in whiteness: the lonely, embarrassing desire to play at self-sufficiency in the face of overwhelming evidence that we are all in fact profoundly interdependent. You can deny that interdependence only by seeing swaths of the people you rely on, and all the land and non-human beings, as unworthy of consideration and relationship. I don't want to do this anymore. There are things white people have that I would like everyone to have, like the benefit and protection of social institutions; the assumption of being capable, kind, and lovable; and serious consideration of their views. But I don't want everyone to have to sign on to the project of whiteness to have to get these things. I think whiteness actually sucks as a way of living.

In an interview in *The Undercommons: Fugitive Planning & Black Study*, the Black cultural theorist Fred Moten describes how a genuine and productive coalition with white people who aspire toward antiracism would have to come from white people's "recognition that it's fucked up for you, in the same way that we've already recognized that it's fucked up for us. I don't need your help. I just need you to recognize that this shit is killing you, too, however much more softly, you stupid motherfucker, you know?"[2] As a stupid motherfucker, this is one of the passages I think of most often when I think of why and how to try and do antiracism as a white person. Again, the ways that racism harms people of colour are more important than the way it harms white people. But as a white person, I don't want to exist in this world in a way where I am denying reality and pretending not to see anyone my way of life harms.

Growing Up in Omàmiwininiwak

The Ottawa Valley, where I grew up, was formed when the Earth's crust shifted downwards between the Mattawa and Petawawa fault zones in the late Precambrian or early Cambrian, hundreds of millions of years ago. Into the depression formed by these movements, a river flowed, known variously as the Kichi-Sìbì, Kitchissippi, Ottawa River, or Rivière des Outaouais.

The Ottawa Valley is claimed as part of Omàmiwininiwak (the territory of the "people living downstream" in Algonquin) and is also currently claimed by the Canadian provinces of Ontario and Quebec. When people arrived from France to colonize these lands, the Voyageurs would paddle canoes (whose English name comes from an Iroquoian word) up the Ottawa River, portaging across rivers and lakes to Georgian Bay. Settlers in the area experienced a boom of wealth from cutting white pine for lumber. By the time I was born there in the mid-1980s the area was overwhelmingly white, rural, and poor.

The Ottawa Valley is covered by the Dish With One Spoon Treaty. When settlers like me to refer to the "Dish With One Spoon Treaty," we tend to mean a specific agreement made between the Anishinaabe and Haudenosaunee nations in 1701, but "Dish With One Spoon," or "One Dish One Spoon," refers not just to that specific treaty but also to a general type or structure of agreement that has been used for at least a millennium to allow multiple nations to agree on how to share the same land.[3] "One Dish One Spoon" means what it sounds like: that we treat the land we live on as though it is a dish we are sharing with everyone else around us, passing a spoon back and forth as we alternate bites, all enjoying and being nourished together.

I've lived almost all my life within the geographical bounds of the Anishinaabe and Haudenosaunee Dish With One Spoon Treaty, from the Ottawa Valley as a child, over to Montreal, to Ottawa for a decade, then back to Montreal. The treaty is considered to bind not only Anishinaabe and Haudenosaunee people but also people of other Indigenous Nations, descendents of European settlers, and newcomers.

I tend to be skeptical and critical of laws, and there are many laws I'm asked to live under that I think are wrong and whose legitimacy I don't recognize. But it's hard to argue with the commonsensical "One Dish One Spoon" approach. And as a white person living on stolen Indigenous land, I feel grateful to be included within an agreement that grants me guidance on how to live as ethically as possible in a place that is profoundly shaped by historical and ongoing violence and displacement. Regardless of how I feel about it, I benefit from that violence and have done so my whole life. Being offered this relationship is something I take seriously.

What does it mean to treat my surroundings as a dish that I am sharing with everyone else around me? As I understand it, it is deeply at odds with many of the things my own culture teaches. If I ask my whiteness what it means to live well and be safe, the answer is to accumulate and hoard. If I want to be safe, I should make money, accumulate savings, and chase and cling to positions of power. I should remove things that belong to all people in common, claim them for my own, and protect them from other people. I should buy a house. I should consider myself distinct from and in competition with the people around me. Safety means protecting myself from other people. Those are not the values I would claim, but they also have their hooks so deep in me that it's difficult to even see how much they've shaped me and to imagine otherwise. And I believe it's the values you live by that matter, not the values you claim. "One Dish One Spoon" offers an alternate vision but when taken seriously — as

I believe it should be — it challenges me to live in a way that is very different from the way I was raised.

I believe it is our relationships that keep us safe. This is hard to square with the knowledge that our relationships also expose us to hurt, harm, uncomfortable growth, opportunities to hurt or harm others, the need to mend relationships, the possibility of fucking up a relationship and being unable to mend it, and many other aspects of the whole mortifying ordeal of being known. Conversely, the money in my bank account won't let me down or let me know when I've broken relationship. The interest on that money might come from building pipelines against the wishes of the caretakers of the land they occupy, or from selling bombs to genocidal governments, but I will be offered every opportunity to pretend the dollars that land in my account come from nowhere, as clean and innocent as new-fallen snow.

What "One Dish One Spoon" means to me is staying aware of the fact that we share space and that everything we have we take from the same finite supply as the other people we're sharing with. It means their needs and desires are exactly as important as mine. There is no way of isolating myself and considering my own needs apart from the communal whole; there is only denying the relationship and working to ignore it. The relationship is always there. If some of the money in my bank comes from the profits that a weapons company makes selling bombs to Israel to drop on Gaza, I am in a relationship with the state of Israel and the people of Gaza. I can try and ignore that relationship, or I can acknowledge it and hold it to the same ethical standards as all of my other relationships.

My thinking on this topic has been shaped by *Becoming Kin: An Indigenous Call to Unforgetting the Past and Reimagining Our Future* by Patty Krawec, an Anishinaabe and Ukrainian writer who belongs to Lac Seul First Nation in Treaty 3 territory. Krawec writes that for people, especially settlers, who would like to begin living in ways other than those colonialism has set out for them, "there is no magic bullet. No single book you can read, no one podcast to listen to, no perfect Twitterati to follow, no percentage you can donate, and no amount of time you can spend outside in nature will put things right. We have to build relationships."[4] She is also one of the founders of the Niikinaaganaa Foundation, which "challenges settlers to pay their rent for living on Indigenous land and then disburses those funds to Indigenous people, meeting immediate survival needs as well as supporting the organizing and community building needed to address the structural issues that create those needs," which I contribute to monthly.[5]

It takes a long time to change your reflexes, especially when it comes to things that you learned early in life and things that you identify with safety and danger. If you, like me, grew up steeped in a white context where you associate safety with self-sufficiency, moving toward interdependency will feel dangerous and frightening. The good news is that you don't have to, and cannot, do it all at once. You can only do it one leap of faith at a time, tying yourself thread by thread back into the world.

TEN

Investing in Shared Resources

> Looking out of my daughter's bedroom window, I can see a grand total of seven different trampolines in back gardens. Almost every family with children has one, of varying sizes and quality. Some are used all the time, some rarely. But it seems to be almost universal now. Every family has its own trampoline. Meanwhile, the playground round the corner falls apart quietly. It's usually empty when we go there. When the swings broke years ago, the council took the frame down rather than replace them.
>
> —JEREMY WILLIAMS, "Every Child on Their Own Trampoline"[1]

In Chapter 9, I described the ideology I grew up in as a white person. It is easy for me to feel that hoarding resources keeps me safe and that relationships, sharing, and acknowledging interdependence put me at risk. But interdependence is a fact of the world. When you're sick, whether you ask a friend to drop off soup, pay restaurant cooks and gig delivery workers to bring you takeout, or drag yourself to the store to buy food grown and processed by agricultural workers, you are depending on other people. You just have the option to use money to pretend you're independent and not in relationship with everyone else in the world.

Those of us who grew up within this ideology have other options though. If you were raised to value and strive toward this fictive independence from others, it will be difficult to acknowledge that no matter what you do you are interdependent with all kinds of people and other living things. It will feel dangerous and humiliating to ask for favours. You may have to remind yourself repeatedly: Don't I feel loved when someone trusts me enough to ask for my help? Don't I want to live in a world where people share what they have and ask favours of one another? Isn't it nicer to shore up your bonds of friendship rather than reinforcing the grim cruelty of the gig economy? It unquestionably is, but you might have to counteract a lot of cultural programming to get there. If it is difficult to ask, it may be easier to offer, to take stock of what you have and could share or what your friends and neighbours need that is within your means to get and share with them.

"Public affluence" is a useful term to describe how much better it makes our lives when we orient toward sharing things rather than some of us having our own and some of us having none. I first encountered the concepts of public affluence and private affluence in Jeremy Williams' essay "Every Child on Their Own Trampoline," which is quoted at the beginning of this chapter. He uses the trampoline example to draw out the difference between private affluence, "individuals gaining things for themselves — possessions, nice homes and experiences, trampolines," and public affluence, "money spent lavishly on things that are shared — libraries, parks, buses, playgrounds."[2] Public affluence is less wasteful and "represents an alternative route to a rich standard of life based on Earth-friendly sociality," according to the socialist urbanist writer Mike Davis.[3]

Ruelles vertes

At its best, Montreal, the city I live in, encourages a sense of public affluence and "Earth-friendly sociality." Most people live in apartments in dense neighbourhoods without a huge amount of private space but within walking distance of a beautiful public park. When the weather is warm the parks are *full* of people eating, drinking, celebrating, reading, hanging out. The city has a program for "*ruelles vertes*" (green alleys), where "*riverains*" (the people whose homes back on to the alley, from a word referring to the people who live along a river) work with their *arondissement* to form a committee to collectively grow plants and add community art and toys, spaces to sit and spend time, and other environmentally sustainable features.[4] The green alley program has expanded into "white alleys" (where neighbours work together to clear the snow from their alley and develop shared winter activities), "blue-green alleys" (where people collect rainwater in rain barrels and rain gardens), and "active alleys" (designed to promote mixed-use spaces for socializing and active use). A 53-page guide from the city steers prospective *riverains* through the process of forming a committee and developing their alley.[5]

There is a lot of ground between bringing a friend soup and making change at the scale of a city. Between those two extremes, there are a lot of fun things you can do to make your life less privatized and more relationship-based.

Open Copy

Late Night Copies Press is a zine-centric press run by Aiden Bettine and India Johnson in Minneapolis. Deciding to share their equipment and knowledge, they began hosting Open Copy at their home two Sundays a month, where they invited people to come use their photocopiers and other zine-making supplies at affordable rates and provided help and advice. The project has since moved out of their home and become the Workshop for Independent Publishing, which now hosts Open Copy.[6]

In their zine about Open Copy, *Own the Means of Production and Share It: Why & How Artists Should Pool Resources*, Johnson describes how they decided to acquire and share equipment, the economics of how it works, and the logistical hurdles they've encountered.[7] The zine lists other resources they've seen artists sharing with their community, including "a scrappy home exhibition venue (clothesline, laundry room, front porch)," a PO box, and getting in on "a bulk order of materials or supplies." The zine is a beautiful, practical tribute to the value of overcoming a scarcity model in the arts, taking an expansive view of what you can share if you take relationships and collectivity, rather than individuality, as your baseline.

I've found it helpful to inventory my resources so I can be more ready to share them. Four of the things I've realized I can and should share:

- The most obvious one is money. My grandparents paid for me to go to university, my dad is a lawyer, I put in almost a decade of working full-time salaried jobs before I stopped being able to do that, and I can still freelance in decently paid work. This means I have a lot more money and access to money than most people in my life. I understand this as giving me a strong responsibility to help friends with money (gifts, never loans), to buy the coffee or food when we go out, to buy people's art, and to pay higher on sliding scales.
- I am white, can often pass as a man if I butch up a bit, and can use all my class privilege to make authority figures feel that I am someone who is, like them, respectable, sympathetic, and deserving. This means I can help people navigate bureaucracies that are inclined to dehumanize them but can be swayed toward treating them more respectfully if I tag along or make a phone call for them.
- I have medically and legally transitioned, and I try to make it known that I'm happy to share any information and experiences I have with anyone to whom it'd be useful, especially since some of the medical interventions I've had aren't the most common ones.
- I started my small press, Sheer Spite, because I'd been making zines for over a decade and I have some specialized skills in layout, production, and distribution, and a lot of relationships within zine worlds. I was already helping other people with these things informally for fun, but I realized that if I called helping people with their books

and zines a small press, I could make the people I helped eligible for things like arts grants and awards. It's silly that it matters whether something was self-published or published through a press, but as long as that's the case, if I can funnel money and legitimacy to people by calling myself a press, I'll do it.

Spend some time thinking about what you have that other people in your life don't, or what you have more of that you might be able to share. It could be something concrete like money, but it might be something less obvious:

- If you have gone through any bureaucratic systems like social assistance (welfare), immigration, or any kind of specialized healthcare, you have knowledge that can help other people so much! How can you make this knowledge more available?
- If you've been in a subculture or scene for a long time, you're in a good position to make sure it is welcoming to other people, especially if they differ in factors like age, race, gender, class, or ability from the bulk of other people in the scene. It feels bad to acknowledge but clout is a real resource, and where you have it, you should be using it to invite people in who might otherwise not be readily welcomed. Introduce them around, show them how things work, and make sure they have a good time.
- Do you have the ability to get out of cities? A lot of people don't! If you have access to a car and/or a place to stay in the country, that's a really precious thing that's nice to share.

- If you have experience with being sick, disabled, or Mad, you have precious knowledge of accommodations, workarounds, meds, treatments, and strategies for navigating and surviving ableism.
- Are you good at shoplifting, scams, dumpster diving, and other criminalized activities? Can you mentor people in those skills who'd really benefit from them, or share your bounty strategically?

In writing this book I often pause and wonder whether I am straying away from the topic of friendship. Or if friendship is a front that I'm using to smuggle in mutual aid? (Yes.) But even if you construe friendship in the most narrow and traditional way, developing your capacity and reflex to provide and accept material assistance will enrich your friendships.

When I spoke to India about Open Copy, she was candid that she spends most of her Saturdays doing Open Copy, has never been paid for it, "and working for free at this pace is unsustainable for me, or probably anyone in the long term." She added, "I guess I'm just interested trying to make something like Open Copy happen at all, but it is kind of a radical thing to do even within the landscape of community printshops … it's really cool that we do it, and it also stretches my energy, time, skills, and money." I am always grateful when people make their skills and resources available and extra grateful when they are honest about how hard it can be. I seem to have also made zines my life's work, and I can confirm that it's wonderful, meaningful, expensive, and exhausting, and that it's hard to imagine what I would do with my time otherwise. I think it's important to approach attempts at resource-sharing, as with many other things, as experiments that can shift in form and scope, change hands, or end when they're no longer working. Having to change or wrap up a project isn't the same as never having tried.

Dick's Lending Library

When a friend told me about Dick's Lending Library, which was then only a few months old, the first thing I said was "I want to be friends with whoever runs that!" Little did I know I was playing right into its founder's scheme to make friends. And now I am their friend, as well as a member of the library's organizing collective. Dick's is a community-run library that specializes in the literary, political, and artistic work of trans, non-binary, and Two Spirit authors.[8] It has an online catalogue where Montrealers can make an account, check out books, and have them delivered by a friendly trans person. Your book might come with a bookmark that encourages you to leave "index cards, fragments of paper, tabs, or post-it notes" in the books you borrow, so that they can "become a site of cruising, longing, critical commentary, reflection, and community."

The library was started by Calev Litvack, a white trans-masculine Montrealer, from their own personal book collection when they realized they had a wealth of trans books and a dearth of community. "I was lonely," they recalled when I asked about their decision to found the library, "and I wanted the books I had to make their way into other people's lives and also for other people's lives to find their way into mine. I thought that if I loosened my attachment to the things I owned, other people might want to do the same with their collections." Started in the early years of the ongoing COVID-19 pandemic, Dick's was a way to build social bonds with a relatively low risk of illness transmission. While it began as a one-person operation, it's now a working collective of about eight regulars (myself included) who work to expand the collection, hold events, and dream about ways the library can grow. It's also achieved its original goal. "I feel so much more connected to community," Calev says, also mentioning that "working and having conversations as a collective has at various points challenged me and pushed me to chill out and step back in ways that feel really good. Sometimes I've felt protective [of the books and the project] but that discomfort is a necessary part of having the library become what it aspires to be."

The library's name came from Litvack's father, Richard, who had a large home library, "a wealth of knowledge" that Calev and their brother "would tiptoe around." It was private, not shared, its contents were a lot different from Dick's' ("it was white man central"), and Richard never went by Dick. "It was inspired by his library but also in opposition to it," Calev told me. Through a private home library you can build precious connections to books and ideas. You may even connect with the books' authors, if you read contemporary writers who are within reach of you socially. But reading and owning books in itself will not usually put you into substantive, living, difficult relationships with others. "The work that we're doing [to run the library] is also a place to build relationships. It feels like the beginning of expanding small networks of care," Calev says. The library is currently fundraising to be able to rent a physical space, which Calev describes as making them feel "so hopeful for just a place to hang out, just pal around, and hopefully connections can develop in that spaces and people can show up for each other in different ways."

They see projects like the library as a complement to trans organizing that's built around emphasizing a sense of urgency in responding to some new crisis or atrocity. While acknowledging the importance of those responses, Calev also spoke about the importance of what they called "the slow work of being there, providing resources, having spaces where people can have fun and chill, while at the same time working to redistribute whatever money we can, in whatever ways we can." Calev told me that they just prefer the slower pace of less urgent community work "that, alongside other forms of organizing, helps create lives worth living." There is a risk to this. I won't say there isn't. I recently spilled water on a book I'd borrowed from Dick's and now it's all bent (sorry Calev). People have borrowed books and not returned them. Starting or taking part in community projects creates an approximately 100% chance that you will deal with conflict, annoyance, flakiness, overcommitment, disappointment, misunderstanding, and general hassle. Personally, I think it is a small price to pay for the pleasure of getting to be in the world with other people, but every single moment won't be a joy and a delight.

Reorienting Toward Relationship

I don't think a lending library, a community photocopier, or an alley with shared garden space are the answers to everything. They do not in themselves pose much of a threat to the established order, but they're a foothold. Maybe you go to Open Copy and the person using the photocopier before you is printing flyers for a demo they're organizing. Maybe a flyer for a weekly community dinner for trans women falls out of your library book on transfeminism. And maybe the neighbour you meet gardening in the *ruelle* has the same terrible landlord as you and is starting a tenant organization.

Is this friendship? I don't think it is, but I think it builds the soil in which friendship can grow. It is also possible to share resources and do cool mutual aid stuff without allowing yourself to be deeply known and cared for and to still be lonely. The built environment you live in — whether it's a dense urban neighbourhood or a spread-out car-oriented suburb — will affect how easy or hard it is to get a project going and make connections, as does the culture of where you live. Some places are chatty and friendly, others are resolutely frosty. Living somewhere it's socially acceptable to talk to strangers has been a factor in my decisions about where to live; I think it matters a lot.

Reorienting from individualism and privatization to relationship and resource-sharing is a huge shift, and you can't do it all in one bite. Community organizers in my life often talk about "moving at the speed of trust." If trust doesn't come easily to you, you can start small. But the important thing is to know what direction you're pointed and keep heading that way.

ELEVEN

Organizing Together

Defend the world in which we win as if it were your child.
It is your child.
Defend it as if it were your lover.
It is your lover.

—AURORA LEVINS MORALES, "V'ahavta"[1]

One of the many things I love about living in Montreal, at least in the circles I spend time in, is that going to protests tends be a great way of catching up with friends. When I'm exchanging "we should get together sometime" texts with pals, one or the other of us often ends up texting a link to the details of a march, vigil, or demo, saying, "I'm planning to go to this, maybe I'll see you there?" In my experience of living here, friendship and political action are tied closely together. I see my friends at meetings, working sessions, in the streets. It both makes it safer and more pleasant to protest and keeps my relationships grounded in our shared values.

Montreal is also very cold for a lot of the year, and knowing I'll see familiar friendly faces — and that they have come in the expectation that I'll also show up — helps get me out the door on a dark January night. Some of my sweetest memories are of sharing winter protests with friends. One weekend there was a winter carnival protest outside the home of Canada's minister of foreign affairs. Demonstrating against her support of Israel's genocide of Palestinians, we played music, read poetry, made ornaments to hang in the trees, and drank hot coffee that steamed frantically in the frigid air.

Solidarity Soup

One of my favourite things I've had the honour of being involved with was Solidarity Soup, an informal collective of friends who made big pots of soup to serve at the end of pro-Palestine marches over the winter of 2023–24. Its founders and heart were a group of Filipinx artists and organizers, including my friend Andi. We brought a card table, big pots of homemade soup wrapped in towels, and thermoses of hot water to help re-heat it and scooped portions into paper cups to put into freezing hands that had been hoisting signs. It was such a joy to keep having the same conversation:

"What's this?"
"Soup!"
"How much is it?"
"Free!"
"Free??"
"Yes! Would you like some?"
"Yes!"

It was so fun to give out soup! It also helped me solidify and build friendships with some of the other soup-makers. And I hope it made it a little easier for people to show up to the marches, which were happening every week throughout the dead of winter, attended at that point after the first flush of protests mainly by people from Arab diasporas, many of whom no doubt had deep personal connection to the atrocities being committed in Gaza and beyond.

The zine *Don't Just Do Nothing: 20 Things You Can Do to Counter Fascism*, compiled by Cindy Barukh Milstein, asks that we "notice the moment when someone comes to understand that food can be good and free and shared without restrictions, obligations, eligibility criteria, or expectations; this means that things don't have to be the way they are."[2] The same zine, which is grounded in Jewish anarchist ethics, suggests, "Make people soup and do not stop inviting them over for soup! Be a reason for living." And there really is something about soup. My friend Garrett Bucks, who writes the newsletter *The White Pages* about community organizing and how to be a more tolerable white person, writes about the Midwestern US tradition of soup and pie suppers and his belief in the central role that communal food-based events play in building "a movement composed of little dots across the country — in small towns and big cities and sprawling exurbs — where people put on events and hold spaces that their neighbors actually want to come back to."[3]

Friendship complements activism, community organizing, and political mobilization so well that I'm not sure how I would separate them from one another. The Black American author, documentarian, and professor Toni Cade Bambara's advice to "make the revolution irresistible" points the way to weaving the most joyful things in life — friendship, food, kids, art — deeply into activism and organizing.[4] Food is a necessity of life. Taking care of people's material needs always makes it easier and nicer for people to show up and makes them feel cared for. It sows conviviality, the gateway to friendship. The document "Some Actions That Are Not Protesting or Voting," compiled by Mariame Kaba, offers many more, often sociable and joyful, ways that you could work to change your community for the better, including cooking and baking for community gatherings (like Solidarity Soup!), organizing reading groups, training and skill-sharing, practising community self-defence, helping escort people to abortion appointments if there are picketers at clinics, participating in a childcare collective, and many more.[5]

Affinity Groups

Affinity groups are a bridge between friendship and organizing, a way of thinking about friendship as a politically organized force. In their zine *How to Form an Affinity Group: The Essential Building Block of Anarchist Organization*," anarchist publisher CrimethInc. describes an affinity group as "a circle of friends who understand themselves as an autonomous political force."[6] While there are undoubtedly parallel formulations based in other cultural traditions, and effaced by colonialism, the lineage of affinity groups that I am familiar with draws on antifascist organizing during and in the lead-up to the Spanish Civil War. There was a pre-existing tradition of small groups of friends, called "*tertulias*" (gatherings), who would meet at cafes to discuss political ideas. When Spanish anarchists became more organized, affinity groups became the building block of their movement.[7]

The term "affinity group" was popularized in North America via the Catalan-American artist Ben Morea, who used it to describe the projects he co-founded, Black Mask and Up Against the Wall Motherfucker.[8] Their Dadaist-inspired work ranged from throwing blood, eggs, and stones at the US secretary of state, to organizing free concerts, to cutting the fences at Woodstock to let people in for free, to potentially being the source of the gun that Valerie Solanas used to shoot Andy Warhol. From there the term spread outwards throughout North American leftist organizing.

Attending actions and demonstrations with others can be important for safety in environments where there the police and other bad actors can be a danger. Affinity groups can be a tool for collective decision-making and accountability around what degree and type of risk you are willing to take, when and how you want to bail, and how to deal with emergencies that arise. If your habit is to only attend marches with a very low risk of arrest and other forms of violence, it's still nice to have plans to meet someone at a march to keep you accountable for showing up. However, as CrimethInc. writes, affinity groups can encompass a much broader range of activities, like organizing "a sewing circle or a bicycle maintenance collective … community gardens … neighborhood childcare programs and wildcat strikes."[9] Affinity groups can function as a bridge between friendship and political organizing.

Throughout his speeches and writing, Dr. Martin Luther King Jr. referred to the idea of "the beloved community," drawn from the work of 19th-century philosopher Josiah Royce.[10] My favourite definition of it comes from the Student Nonviolent Coordinating Committee, an organization that mobilized students in the 1960s Black civil rights movement in the US, which described the beloved community as a "circle of trust, a band of sisters and brothers gathered around the possibilities of agapeic love" and cited it as the reason many people began to engage with direct action.[11]

"Agape" is a term from Christian ancient Greek, which refers to the love the Christian God has for humanity and humanity's love for God, which extends as well to our fellow humans. I am not a Christian, but I admire the thread in Christianity, as in most other religions, where caring for the material needs of all your fellow people is considered intrinsic to religious devotion. C.S. Lewis wrote that each friendship "is a pocket of potential resistance. Men [sic] who have real friends are less easy to manage or 'get at'; harder for good Authorities to correct or for bad Authorities to corrupt."[12] We have seen that as people grow lonelier, we also grow more susceptible to recruitment into hate movements. The more time you spend serving soup at protests, the less time you have to sit at your computer alone going down YouTube rabbit holes. And each cup of soup is a tiny thread linking you to whomever reaches out for one.

TWELVE

Planning Together

By expanding our relationships and embracing interdependence, we can leverage power against the threats we face and extend care amid crisis. We can courageously reach out and connect with other people, even if we feel like we don't have much in common with them. When we experience a taste of collective power, our courage will grow, as we recognize that we are stronger together and that we are not alone.

—KELLY HAYES AND MARIAME KABA, *Let This Radicalize You: Organizing and the Revolution of Reciprocal Care*[1]

At the start of the COVID-19 pandemic my conception of preparedness was individualistic: I wanted to be able to seal myself away as completely as possible from the living, breathing community around me as I suddenly became terrified of the danger our breath posed to one another. I stocked up on non-perishable foods and went out as little as possible. I was as miserable and lonely as I have ever been.

A few years later I was living in downtown Ottawa during the trucker convoy, a six-week occupation of the city by alt-right protesters. I saw a lot of racist, white supremacist symbols being proudly displayed in my neighbourhood. I learned that in a lot of situations my whiteness protects me more than my queerness or transness endangers me. I experienced the joy and relief of being able to *do something*: to lend the shelter of my whiteness and my ability to pass as male and as abled to my neighbours by walking with them on errands through a gauntlet of fascists.

Recently, a school board building near where I live now in Montreal was the site of a planned rally against acknowledging the existence of trans people. These happen a lot, but one being held right in my neighbourhood activated the damage I hold from the trucker convoy, so I left and stayed with a friend elsewhere. The transphobes got wildly out-organized that day: a sad handful of creeps faced with a big happy crowd of trans people, but I was still grateful for the ability to skip out. It sparked conversations with friends that led to a couple of us making copies of our apartment keys for one another in case any of us needed to get away quickly and stay somewhere else for a bit. Right-wing movements are feeling increasingly empowered everywhere. The climate crisis is accelerating: freak storms will bring down parts of the power grid or flood neighbourhoods, wildfire smoke will be worse in some places than others, and we will all need the ability to leave our homes quickly and have somewhere else to go. And at any time, a romantic or roommate relationship can turn bad in a hurry and make your home unsafe.

The mainstream vision of preparedness tends, unsurprisingly, toward individualism: having a bunker to retreat to, having a stockpile of food for you and your family, and having guns and the fantasy of using them to protect what's yours. In addition to being unrealistic for the types of problems I am likely to face, guarding a mountain of MREs with a shotgun is not a fantasy with much appeal for me. I'll be better served for most situations by having keys to friends' apartments in other neighbourhoods and maintaining strong relationships with my friends in other cities in case any of us needs to go sleep on someone else's couch for a bit.

Having somewhere else to go is also just nice for non-emergency situations! I'm writing this chapter from a friend's spare room, where I'm staying because my roommate's family are in town for Passover. None of us can really afford a hotel room easily, so staying with my friend gives them space to hang out as a family, lets her mom sleep in my bed instead of on a couch that hurts her back, and also lets me manage my COVID risk budget. It's also a joy to have a few days of slumber party with my friend! I feel like a lot of adults yearn for the kinds of multi-day hangouts they enjoyed as kids or teenagers, but you can just do that. And the more you feel comfortable going and sleeping on a friend's couch, the less you will hesitate to invite yourself over if your power goes out or your partner starts acting scary. This kind of preparedness is minimal: just an exchange of spare keys and an openness to sleepovers. Something like that can also be an entry point into larger conversations about preparing with your friends to weather life's uncertainties together.

Group Preparedness Planning

Transition US and NewStories, two organizations aimed at building capacity for community action and transformation, created the free online guide *Ready Together: An Emergency Preparedness Handbook for You and Your Neighbors.*[2] It's a workbook designed to be done with neighbours to make plans for getting through things together, such as by making meetup plans and figuring out how to meet your needs for food, water, and other essentials together.

My friend Meghan met monthly with a group of eight friends to work through *Ready Together* over potluck dinners. While that group had existing relationships with one another, Meghan is now in the process of convening another group who are all neighbours but who don't know each other well yet. She explained, "I'm bringing together some specific folks in specific situations that I want to understand better what they need," including new immigrants from the Congo, working-class single older women who don't drive, older people who have been in the neighbourhood a long time, and families with young kids. Some of the friends from the first group are now also forming planning circles with other people in their lives.

When I asked her about her entry points into community preparedness, she explained that she had grown up living communally in an intentional community. As a child, she sometimes found it frustrating to live in an income-sharing community because it meant that she often couldn't have class signifiers like name-brand shoes or salon haircuts. As she grew up, she realized that her family's decision to forgo those and share their resources allowed for things like her friend's disabled parent to have health insurance and a physically accessible home. She acknowledged that, in practice, trading in middle-class comforts so that other people can be allowed to survive — what's sometimes known as "living simply so that others may simply live" — is a hard sell even for people who see ourselves as compassionate anti-consumerists. But ultimately she identifies interdependence as "the orientation that feels the best in my body" even and especially in times of stress and crisis.

By working through the preparedness guide, Meghan and her friends were able to find out the most likely form of disaster in their region (flood), make plans for what they would do in that event, and figure out what supplies (hip waders) would be useful to have in advance. The process also served as a form of political education: one member of the group used a Freedom of Information request to access their region's emergency plan for flooding (there wasn't one). The group began to build power at the local level for political action around infrastructure, advocating for their region's emergency response systems to be improved, better resourced, and made more just.

The process also helped the group knit their friendships closer on a day-to-day basis outside of huge catastrophes. "It moved me and those relationships toward more explicit consideration of how we would care for each other in real life." She commented that it made it easier for members of the group to stop by and help each other in a more spontaneous, comfortable way.

The prospect of having friends drop by unexpected is a weirdly contentious one. I often see people express nostalgia for times in their life, like university, when it was easier for friends to spend time together spontaneously, not doing anything formal, just hanging out, doing whatever they would be doing alone, but together. However, I have also heard a surprising amount of people express a belief that there is something fundamentally creepy about visiting someone spontaneously, whether they're a friend or a neighbour they don't yet know, and that there must be something else sinister underlying the motives of anyone who would do such a perverse thing. When Meghan and I talked about this phenomena, she said,

> I'm curious what is terrifying about having someone drop by. What bad thing could happen? Oftentimes I see it as a desire to not be inconvenienced, but convenience is one of those luxuries that have to go, when it comes to actually being interdependent and being part of a community of care that you can rely on. Yeah. It'll fucking inconvenience you. And you know what, let it. Because you'll find new life after inconvenience.

My friend Imogen pointed to something similar when I was talking to her about friendship:

> Friendship needs to be something you have to constantly work at. It takes effort. And we don't want it to take effort. We don't want it to be messy. We want it to be neat and tidy, and we want it to conform with our timeframe, and we want it to be on our schedule, and we want it to always be in the background until we need it in the foreground.

Both of these conversations stuck in my mind, and I'm grateful to these friends for making the tension between convenience and interdependence so clear. Valuing convenience will pull you away from interdependence. It will always be more convenient to do things yourself or pay other people to do them on your precise terms, exactly when and how you want. If you get food delivered you will get what you want, when you want it, by an anonymous person who will leave it outside your door without speaking to you, if that's what you request. However, if you let a friend know that you're sick, or sad, or broke, and could use a hot meal, it will be inconvenient. They might stop by with food, but they'll have to fit it in around the rest of their life, and the food might not be exactly what you would have chosen, and worst of all, you will be drawn further into a relationship with them. They will know that you aren't doing well. They might want to know what's going on. You will be perceived. There is a possibility that you will annoy or frustrate them. You will owe them one and have an obligation to keep an eye out for when they're in need and you can return the favour, whether or not it happens to be a good time for you. All of this is extremely inconvenient. It is also what makes life worth living.

Meghan also pointed out the contradiction that while some of us may see it as inconvenient for friends to drop by unexpectedly, we generally don't frame things like the demands our jobs place on us as an inconvenience. What could be less convenient than having to show up for work, no matter how you feel about it or what else you have going on? But I have rarely heard work spoken of in those terms. Work feels mandatory, work holds the power of life and death over us. As we saw in Chapter 8 though, it is possible to move work a little further from the centre of our lives. It is worth considering whether you might let your friendships inconvenience you a fraction as much as your job does.

What Do We Owe to People We Don't Like?

When I talk about friendship as a bridge into mutual aid and interdependence, I want to be clear that I don't mean closing ranks. We can start by strengthening our existing relationships with people we love and trust, but we can't end there. "Even bad people deserve to survive the apocalypse," as Meghan put it, clarifying immediately that she doesn't believe in categorizing people as good or bad, that "none of this is permanent, including your goodness or your badness, my goodness or my badness." She identifies an obsession in right-wing prepping with deciding "who's in and who's out": who will be allowed to live in the case of a survival scenario. The people who are "out" are disproportionately disabled people and elders, those who are unable to do heavy physical labour. You might allow someone you hate to partake of your resources if they can prove themselves useful enough. And someone who isn't considered "useful" may be suffered to live if someone with resources loves them. But what about people who you don't like and who also aren't "of use" to you in any obvious way?

I read and think obsessively about the AIDS crisis and its legacies. Whether it's visible or not, it underpins my writing and the way I think about the world. One thread that runs through a lot of writing about AIDS from the depths of the Western AIDS crisis is the necessity of caring for people you dislike. If the most annoying person you know is shitting themself to death and they do not have anyone else to clean them up and make sure they drink some water, guess what? You have to do it! I think about a lot about the combination of love and bitchiness, bitterness, and burnout that runs through AIDS writing — you have a duty of care not just to people you like or think are fun or cute.[3]

It probably becomes clearer in a sweeping crisis like AIDS was before effective treatment and prevention were developed, but are we not now in a crisis of poverty, suicide and social murder among trans people? What do I owe the peers I dislike? How can I infrastructuralize my care and make it go as far as it can when I am only one person and am stretched thin caring for the people I actively love? For me the answer is to develop skills of care and interdependence in my friendships and try to bring them into other milieus that are better suited to provide care at scale. I look at that in the next chapter, which talks about how our friendships can help us learn to repair a relationship.

What Does It Look Like to Plan with Your Friends?

If you live long enough, your friends will start getting sick, becoming disabled or more and differently disabled, and dying. This time will come at different phases in your life depending on who you're in community with, but it will come. If you live in communities that experience a lot of trauma, people you know will kill themselves, and others will think about it. You will end up on some late-night visits or phone calls or hospital waiting room excursions.

I wrote above about ways that married people, or even cohabitating couples, are privileged socially over singles. There is not much any of us can individually do to overcome these structural problems, but in a lot of cases we can work around them by building our own plans and infrastructure. Planning for one another's hospitalization, sickness, and disability is crucial among these. When we plan together in smaller, less fraught ways, we work up to planning together in these larger, heavier ways. Here are some ways to prepare together, ordered approximately by difficulty:

- *Get extra:* If you can, pick up extra COVID tests, masks, HRT, emergency supplies, food that's on sale, or food you dumpstered, and make it known that you're happy to share. Tell your friends, tell your neighbourhood Facebook group, put up posters, drop things in free boxes, bring them to events.
- *Make an emergency kit:* Spend some time putting together a box of things to bring to a sick friend before there's any sick friend. It could have some juice, a can of soup, some bags of herbal tea, a comic or zine to read, and some chocolate or cookies for a treat. Talk to your friends about it; let them know that you'd love to have an opportunity to bring it to them.
- *Make copies of your keys:* With the consent of the other members of your household, make four or five copies of your keys and give them out to people you trust, ideally in exchange for copies of their keys. That way they can stop by and water your plants or feed your cat if you're out of town, come close your windows if it starts raining while you're at

work, or maybe even just leave you a little treat if they're passing by on the way back from the bakery.

- *Plan fun things together:* If you've planned a trip with friends, you know how complicated planning things with other people can be. But conversely, if you can figure out renting a cottage with five friends, you already have a lot of the skills and groundwork to figure out together what you'd do if your city was on fire. Planning fun things with your friends is good practice and it's also just really nice! I've loved learning about the Korean tradition of *gyemoim*, group savings plans where friends each put in small amounts of money every month and decide together what they'll spend it on, like going on a vacation together.[4]
- *Strategize for emergencies:* A good first step is to identify what the most likely disasters are where you live, because they're probably only going to get worse and more frequent. From there figure out what your group should have on hand when a disaster happens. Whether it's fascist protests, wildfire smoke, flooding, or whatever is a risk in your area, make plans to keep each other safe.
- *Plan for mental health crises:* The writer and therapist carly boyce wrote a wonderful zine called *helping your friends who sometimes wanna die maybe not die*, which is free to read online.[5] The zine is based on their experiences with suicide intervention trainings that failed to account for how "oppression (misogyny, racism, transphobia, homophobia, ableism, colonialism) plays a huge role in not only who is at

risk of wanting to die or dying by suicide but also who gets access to support and services around suicidal risk." boyce "wanted to have conversations with folks who didn't want to call the cops on their pals, or were supporting people who had already had really awful or harmful experiences in emergency rooms and psych wards, about how we show up for our loved ones and communities when people are thinking about leaving this world." The result was a workshop they developed called *suicide intervention for weirdos, freaks, and queers.*[6] Both the workshop and the zine go through common misconceptions about suicidality and how to address it and offer practical strategies for supporting suicidal people.

- *Planning for health emergencies and death care:* Talk to your friends about their access needs, what they need when they're sick/er, how you could help each other if one of you is hospitalized, and your wishes around death and end-of-life care.

I'm in favour of being proactive about planning with friends, but realistically, you probably won't start making this type of serious plan together until something difficult and frightening happens. For my friend Hannah, a white cis queer woman in her 30s, this moment came when a neighbour knocked on her door after experiencing domestic violence. Her neighbour's partner was arrested, Hannah was called to testify based on what she'd heard and witnessed, and ultimately the neighbour's partner was jailed. Hannah was faced with the prospect of not knowing when he would be released, but knowing that when he was, he would be back in her neighbourhood with a history of violence and a reason to have a grudge against her. Understandably, she was afraid.

Hannah's close friend Erica helped Hannah make a safety plan in the form of an elaborate flow chart that would help her make quick decisions in the case of several possible scenarios. The people involved were all renamed in the safety plan after characters from *The Wind in the Willows*, and it was decorated with illustrations from the story, to help defuse the intensity of the situation. The plan helped Hannah think through not only her own physical safety but also how to balance that with her own values. Most of the safety advice she received centred on calling the police, which she wanted to avoid if at all possible. Instead, her plan relied on a network of friends and neighbours to help look out for her. When she did need to put her safety plan into action, she already had go-bags for herself and her cats in her car, a friend to look after the cats, and a place to go. As she recalls it, "I was so upset, but because we'd had so many conversations, and they agreed to this ahead of time, and had been really keen for me to show up. It made me feel like, maybe it is OK to ask for help, and to show up as a mess sometimes." Having existing plans with her friends not only helped Hannah make hard decisions under pressure, it also helped her feel more comfortable relying on her friends in a vulnerable, emotionally intense moment. While she still worried about inconveniencing her friends, having approached them for help ahead of time assured her that they were happy to have her back.

The thing is, it often isn't inconvenient or unpleasant to help your friends, but sometimes it is, and that's OK. Doing the right thing is famously not always easy or immediately pleasant! As you enmesh your life more deeply with others' lives, your norms and reactions will change and interdependence will become easier. Sometimes it will still be annoying to be asked for help and scary to ask. If your notion of safety is predicated on self-reliance, it is hard to shift to thinking of safety as being deeply intertwined with other people. But like all binaries, it's fake. I always keep emergency food in my room and in my backpack, ready to hole up or bolt, in addition to any plans I make with other people. You don't have to make changes all at once, and it's not even possible to. You can keep your hoard of snacks while also starting to plan with your friends and neighbours.

Moving away from lonely convenience toward annoying inconvenient interdependence is difficult and probably a lifelong journey. We'll all need to figure out how to be around people we don't know and people we don't like, to help them out, and to stand in solidarity with their struggles. We'll need to build and sustain institutions and organizations beyond the scale and longevity of individual friendships. And it will be hard, hard, hard. But your friends are people you already like. You've already chosen each other and built trust with one another. Strengthening your capacity for care and interdependence with your friends will stand you in good stead for extending your care outwards and being in community.

THIRTEEN

Learning How (and Why) to Repair

> Figuring out how to live together is hard. To exist in community with people who constantly piss you off is exhausting, but ultimately: worth it … I suppose that's just how you get through, with other people, because the only way to get through is with other people.
>
> —BRYN KELLY, "Diving into the Wreck"[1]

One of my friends has been a long-time organizer with a project that connects incarcerated 2SLGBTQ+ people with penpals outside prisons. Many years ago they told me something that I've thought about ever since. They said that young outside penpals frequently asked the organization if they could be connected with an inside correspondent who was, like them, perhaps a nonbinary transmasculine grey-ace person. Or that they were unsure how to engage with someone who described herself as a tranny or a homosexual or some other word that they'd learned was objectionable and that nobody in the outside penpal's social world used.

I think it'd be easy to hear this and laugh at the younger person. It sure feeds right into boring transphobic tropes about people's increasingly specific and arcane identities. I am not here to make fun of anyone, but there's a reason this passing comment stuck in my mind. I long deeply for friendships with people, especially but not only other 2SLGBTQ+ people who are a generation or more older than I am. I wish I had more people in my life who have seen their friends get sick and die. I don't wish that on anyone, obviously, but when it happens to me, I want to have people to talk to about it who have something to say other than "that sounds really hard." I don't want to have to reinvent every wheel.

To have and to keep those friendships I'll need to always be working on my ability to connect to people who are different from me, from their language on down. And I'll also need to work on my ability to repair breaches in relationships. I believe these two traits to be closely linked. Difference increases the likelihood of small breaches: misunderstandings, miscommunications, differences of opinion, experiences the other didn't share and may not be able to understand, different ways of expressing hurt and care, the list goes on forever. If you want to spend time with people different from you, you have to be capable of repair.

As a millennial queer person, I was taught that the language you use about yourself and ask others to use about you matters a lot, maybe more than anything. I came into queerness believing that if someone used the wrong pronoun for someone or an outdated term, they could not be trusted, taught, or redeemed. Coming into a queer scene that puts such a laser focus on using the right words to describe people and identities above all else is not conducive to learning to work across difference of any kind, and it really did a number on me that I'm working to undo.

Kat, a white trans woman in her 30s, told me about entering queer community in the mid-2010s via a queer summer camp for young adults and how that led her to sever her ties with her working-class Albertan family of origin because they didn't have all the right politics and use all the right language. Over the following years she noticed how that ethos played out for the community leaders who taught it to her: the people who were most strict about the necessity of cutting people out of your life predictably burned through friendships quickly. It took time for her to rebuild relationships with her family of origin, which are still often frustrating but are precious to her nonetheless.

A lot of other people in my life have become estranged from their families and stayed there. People in my life have gone through conversion therapy; physical, sexual, and spiritual abuse; plain neglect and indifference. I'd never argue that everyone needs to be in contact with their family of origin or that it's always fruitful or even possible. But being in a demographic where so many people have severed their ties to their families of origin or have been cut loose from them contributes to the tenor of many of the queer social groups I've been in and their attitudes toward the possibility of repair. As my friend River put it,

> First, I was treated as disposable by my own family and had to repeatedly cut people off for my own existential survival. Then there were more waves: "I'm

> queer." "Oops, queer and trans." "Oops, queer, trans, and sick." Each of those things is another big social filter that many people just can't pass through. And in communities where everyone has different versions of this trauma and the stakes of everything are so heightened, everything becomes a referendum on your worth. It's easy to decide that the thing you need to do is cut people out. Because a solid 50% of the time, it actually has been the thing you needed to do.

Sometimes severing bonds and ending relationships is the right choice, and sometimes repairing them is the right choice. As with most things there are self-evident extremes and a huge murky middle. I've become curious about some of the social factors that push us away from repair, toward cutting ties.

No Good Alone

Rayne Fisher-Quann's viral 2023 essay "no good alone" observes a consensus amongst the theoretically disparate online realms of "hyper-capitalist motivation videos, pseudo-spiritual tweets, and Instagram therapy infographics."[2] Despite their different trappings all of them urge us "to 'focus on yourself,' to 'protect your peace,' to sever relationships that don't serve you and invest your newfound time and energy into self-improvement." They repeat, as discussed earlier, that we don't owe anyone anything. Ultimately, she argues, the fantasy is that if we work hard enough, go to therapy, and excise all our messy neediness, we can opt out of ever again being hurt or hurting others. I also find this fantasy alluring: I would love it if it were that simple. But we live in this world together, and we are going to bump into each other, step on each other's toes, and hurt each other's feelings. And the solutions to those hurts and slights will require us to engage with one another, not to retreat into our own cocoons of self-optimizing healing.

Even people who intellectually believe in collective power, the necessity of revolutionary change, and resistance to oppression are still susceptible to the impulse that healing, rest, and contentment reside in time alone, not in nourishing our bonds with others. I know that because it's something I personally struggle with. I find it so easy to get caught in a vicious cycle where I feel exhausted and burnt out, and it feels like the answer to that is to spend more time alone, because it's easier and it seems more restful. And sometimes that's what you need to restore your peace. But often you'd be better served and more replenished by spending time with people you care about and who care about you. Like my friend Meghan describes in Chapter 8, our desires are not always as reliable a guide as we'd like them to be.

Ayesha Khan describes this pull in an instantly recognizable way in their essay "You Don't Need to 'Fill Your Cup First' to Seek or Be in Community."[3] Ultimately, they argue, it's when you feel most burnt out and most drawn to numbing out in front of a screen or two, that you would be best served by seeking out connection instead. It's a hard sell, I know. I am as susceptible as anyone to the siren song of lying down half-watching a YouTube video while answering emails on my phone. I'm sad and tired and I want pleasure, and I'm frantic from a day's work and can't turn off the pull to accomplish things. But the more time you spend numbing out, the more your relationships and your skill at and inclination toward building and maintaining them wither.

The only thing that helps me extricate myself bit by bit from this cycle is making a point to ask myself and notice when I feel happy and replenished by staying home and playing computer games alone (sometimes!) and how I feel when I go see a friend instead (mostly, but not always, more energized and content). I'm cognizant of not wanting to write "screen bad," which is the absolute least interesting take imaginable. For what it's worth, I do think phones are mostly bad, but the phones are not the problem. If we did not live in neoliberal hell world, phones might be fine.

Who is served when we respond to pain and difficulty by withdrawing from one another, cutting ties, declining to repair frayed or ruptured bonds? Fisher-Quann's essay, quoted above, identifies that becoming suspicious of organic social bonds allows care to be sold to us by therapists and therapy-adjacent apps and services. The hollowing-out of our ability to repair isn't a plot from Big Therapy to sell more therapy though — it's our old friend neoliberalism again. In colonial Canada, we have added decades of concerted attacks on all forms of social safety nets and collective power onto a base of WASP individualism. The combination of these forces push people toward feeling ashamed at the prospect of needing anything from anyone and suspicious of anyone asking anything of them. In researching this book, I stumbled across an article by a "positive psychology-based life coach who writes and speaks on the importance of friendship," who argued that "while extricating yourself from toxic friendships is vitally important, eliminating even mildly negative relationships is advisable too."[4] Stuff like this keeps me up at night: I do not want to live in a world where I have social permission to cut anyone out of my life who I find "even mildly negative."

There is a cultural thread asking us to deal with anything difficult on our own and telling us that when we can't, the morally correct decision is to put it in the hands of a paid professional, whether it's navigating an emotional crisis, moving apartments, or getting food when we're sick and hungry. Scratch a cultural insistence that it is most morally correct to function primarily as an individual and a consumer, and you'll usually find neoliberal economic forces just underneath. When there is moral virtue assigned to being able to pay for everything we need from another person, there is a corresponding implicit moral condemnation of not having the money to pay for everything and relying on interpersonal relationships instead. We all have needs, but having needs and being poor is unacceptable. This ideology is taking hold at a time when 30% of people in Canada are having to reduce their spending on core needs like food and heating for financial reasons: surely, a time when it would be better to draw closer and help one another out.[5]

The difficulty of repair also comes from all the other material factors I've written about elsewhere in this book. People are not doing well. Most people I know are not able to reliably access healthcare, let alone support for their well-being, whether that's therapy, cultural healing practices, time out of the city, or just a day off. We are eating whatever's on sale. We are suffering weird post-viral illnesses that doctors won't take seriously where the only help forthcoming is people commiserating deep in Reddit threads. We are marinating in dread watching multiple genocides unfold online. How could we possibly be expected to extend a generous hand out to people who have hurt us?

If everything in your life is tenuous, it is much harder to go out on a limb and say "Hey, I think I fucked up," or "Hey, you hurt me." It is hard to admit to a mistake when you've seen other people lose their housing and end up homeless when they fuck up. People who are broke and scared and don't have a backup plan are strongly incentivized to find a reason that the other person was wrong, not them, so they can hold tight to what they have.

Deserving Care

Another reason I personally have failed to repair breaches in my relationships is because I've simply never thought of myself as the kind of person who gets to have enduring close relationships. When I am happy in a relationship, part of me is always waiting for the other shoe to drop and for things to get bad or end. When they do, I am all too quick to say, "OK, that was nice while it lasted but now it's time to get back to the natural order of things, where I am alone." Instead of fighting for the relationship, it's easy for me to assume people are better off without me around and to allow our relationship to end.

In his 2017 essay "The Epidemic of Gay Loneliness," Michael Hobbes describes a young man who was talking about "the exact moment he decided to go into the closet" in the late 2000s. "He must have been 10 or 11, dragged on a vacation to Long Island by his parents. 'I looked around at our whole family, and the kids running around, and I thought, 'I'm never going to have this,' and I started to cry.'"[6] Hobbes had felt the same grief around the same age, but in the early 1990s, and interviewed a man who had a strikingly similar experience in the late 1970s. What does it do to gay men — from three different generations — to firmly believe from childhood that there is a type of normative widespread happiness from which they'll be shut out? The researchers that Hobbes talks to about it cite a common pattern among gay men of emotional avoidance, numbness, struggles with emotional vulnerability, difficulty with decision-making around risk, and having sex they don't really want or feel good about.

I can also relate to the feeling that Hobbes and his interviewees described. I've known I was both some type of queer and many kinds of weird since I was a small child, and I've had a strong sense that there were a lot of "normal" things that would never happen for me. In many ways I'm fine with that — a lot of those things I don't want and think are generally detrimental to human thriving. Being shut out from "normal life" offers both liberation to seek other ways of being and a deep sense of shame and loss. In general, trauma also tends to beget black-and-white thinking. There are two kinds of people, them and me. You're Good until you fuck up, then you're Bad. These narratives are not conducive to repair, which requires you to hold several pieces of nominally conflicting information in your head at once, such as "I made a mistake and hurt someone" and "People care about me and want me around."

To learn from childhood that you're a different kind of entity who is shut out of the usual paths to happiness and safety and to experience reinforcement of that notion through violence, exclusion, scorn, and constant low-level fear and discomfort do not incline people toward the expansive thinking and tolerance for discomfort that are required for repair. Being gay is only one axis among many on which people can come to learn they don't deserve all the fruits of human care; it's just one that I happen to be able to vouch for. But it isn't a surprise to me that the queer friend groups I've moved through are marked by rupture and intractable conflict. My impulses in those directions come from the bone-deep shame that's been with me longer than I can remember.

All of this is at play while the stakes of friendship in queer and trans communities can be incredibly high. As my friend Imogen put it, "I think with trans women particularly, friendship is incredibly important. With a lot of trans women, social death means death. If you lose your social circle you die. And I know that sounds dramatic but sometimes all we have is our friends." We need each other so badly, and it will only become less and less possible to survive without a network of strong flexible bonds that can be repaired when they fray or break. What does repair look and feel like?

When I talked about repair to my friend Meghan, who we heard from in Chapter 12, she told me that as a white person she looks to the leadership of Indigenous communities, in particular an example from the Alaska Native community. In communities strongly marked by generational trauma from colonization, including residential schools, there are often high rates of domestic violence and sexual assault. Meghan spoke about admiring the ways that people in those communities have found to keep the most vulnerable community members, especially children, safe while choosing not to ostracize and shun those who have caused harm. In the video *A Healing Journey for Alaska Natives*, community members like Elsie R. Boudreau, who is Yup'ik and president of the organization Arctic Winds Healing Winds, and others from Yup'ik, Athabascan, and Asa'carsarmiut communities speak to a fundamental sense of the interconnectedness of people and of people within the rest of the world.[7] Despite suffering the effects of generational trauma, these communities have managed to maintain a worldview that refuses to see people as individual disposable units. The video profiles programs where men who have committed sex offences are given pathways back into their communities, such as by fishing to provide food for the community.

Ways of Attending to Complexity

Sins Invalid, a performance project led by disabled artists and centred around disability justice, writes beautifully about relationships and collaboration across difference in a section of their book *Skin, Tooth, and Bone: The Basis of Movement Is Our People* called "Why We Commit to Mixed Ability Organizing." They identify that working together across difference "means paying attention to and being honest about the complexities of being in a body, and developing practices capable of attending to that complexity." I think that "attending to complexity" is a lovely way to describe the work required to build and sustain relationships with people who have different needs, experiences, and expectations than you do, a process that involves curiosity, experimentation, and ongoing attention and maintenance. Some of the ways I've found of attending to the complexity of being in the world with other people are time, expanding what you are willing to feel, and changing your relationship to shame.

Time

First on the list is time, because it's easiest: it happens no matter what. I am by no means an elder; I'm in my late 30s. Nevertheless, I've seen my perspective on conflict shift just by having opportunities to see more of people's lives over time. People who I felt certain were, to their core, a particular way, have changed completely. I have felt myself to be, to my core, a particular way, then changed completely. As a younger person I knew in theory that no person or situation is fixed and immutable, but as I get older I see firsthand how much change people are capable of, including myself. It makes me more inclined to be curious where someone is at, how they got there, and where they're going. Time compounds when you can stay put in a geographic location or social milieu and have more opportunities to see the full arc of conflicts amongst people and of the rise and fall of projects and spaces.

Studying history is another great way to get to observe cycles playing out. When I did an internship at the Queer Zine Archive Project, I found it so funny and poignant how many queer and trans zines have contained glossaries on which language is good to use about gender and sexuality and which is bad. Needless to say, there was no consensus. It made me think of all the conflicts I had seen over language, and I realized we've been having those same arguments forever and maybe always will. I'm a writer so obviously I think language matters a lot, particularly when it comes to self-identification. But it is abundantly clear that it is not a realm that will ever yield answers that are correct for all time. It's instead something that will always be contested and where thoughtful people will arrive at different conclusions.

Expanding What You Are Willing to Feel

I love the way Elise Granata put it in her essay "Community Is about What We Are Willing to Feel": "The feelings needed to fully and sustainably participate [are] courage, optimism, trust, love, intimacy, curiosity." She describes how prioritizing these feelings can give us "the resilience to push through the inevitable feelings of fear, overwhelm, frustration, and hurt. The stamina to go through cycles of all of these feelings and more, again and again, and continue showing up even still."[8]

Repair requires the ability to feel bad for a while and to stay there on purpose. It requires accepting that not everyone loves you and sometimes you are careless, unkind, and annoying. There have been more times in my life than I'd like to admit when I have let relationships drop instead of trying to work through conflict and hurt, because I felt like I had maxed out my ability to tolerate pain. Everything else just felt so hard that I couldn't imagine voluntarily putting myself through more discomfort and difficulty. Finding the wherewithal to be honest and hopeful and try to work through conflict is simply harder when you're stressed, broke, sick, in pain, working a shitty job, navigating a racist society, trying to help family overseas who are in danger, or simply observing the rising tide of fascism at home.

If repairing relationships and navigating conflict are skills you haven't practised, then they won't feel possible. By practising honesty and compassion in interactions that feel lower stakes, you can figure out how to hold fast in harder situations. That skill is a gift you can give yourself.

Tolerating Shame and Claiming Bad Kin

If we want to get better at repair, it brings me no pleasure to tell you that the main feeling we (especially my fellow white people) need to expand our capacity to tolerate is shame. Shame is a deeply powerful feeling that can hook into some of our earliest, deepest, and most painful memories like no other. But when we can face what is most hateful and shameful to us about ourselves, we are better positioned to forgive others and to repair breaches in our relationships.

One text around this subject that I think of often is Alexis Shotwell's essay "Claiming Bad Kin."[9] Shotwell is a professor at Carleton University in Ottawa and writes often and thoughtfully about whiteness. In "Claiming Bad Kin" Shotwell writes about the impulse that some progressive white people have when confronted with anti-Indigenous violence perpetrated by white people and other aspects of our complicity in genocide: we often try and disavow or distance ourselves from whiteness. Shotwell, instead, is interested in

> what it could mean for white people and settlers more generally who benefit from historical and current effects of enslavement, colonialism, border militarism, racial distributions of environmental devastation, and capitalism to claim kin with the people producing these effects. If we are complicit in the pain of this suffering world, how might we take responsibility for our bad kin?

Shotwell argues that settlers can't simply take up "Indigenous practices of relationality." Like my friend Meghan suggests, we can listen to and learn from Alaskan Natives about how they live out their values of interconnectedness and repair, but we can't just copy and paste it into our own lives. In Patty Krawec's *Becoming Kin*, mentioned in Chapter 9, she writes about the concept of kinship as specifically not being a series of identical relationships among interchangeable people: "It carries specific responsibilities depending on the kind of relationship we agree upon. An aunt has different responsibilities than a brother."[10] So kinship, and moving into better kinship, with everyone around us — including people we share a lot of identities and experiences with, people whose lives have been a lot different from our own, the land, and other more-than-human beings — means thinking and talking and listening about how we are situated relative to one another, how our lives are bound together and woven within larger, often deeply violent and painful histories, and how we can shift those relationships without denying these histories.

As white people grapple with whiteness and all that it makes us complicit in, we must figure out, as Shotwell puts it, "how to be situated in relation to whiteness in ways that do not disavow or evade its past and present, while simultaneously working toward a future in which more beings than white children have any kind of future at all." White people need to look with clear eyes at our whiteness and all the work it does for us in the world and at whose expense. To be traitors to whiteness, white people need to acknowledge that whiteness claims us and awards us its benefits. White supremacists will still claim us as kin, regardless of our politics. In Shotwell's account, when we acknowledge these things, we are better situated to practise "political friendship or comradeship" across difference.

Shame never pushes me toward building or mending relationships; it pushes me toward closing the door and playing computer games. But when I am able to look clearly at what evokes shame in me, whether it is something I've individually fucked up or broader ways that ease and comfort in my life are built on the suffering of others, I can make choices about it. Choosing to turn toward the pain opens the possibility of repair.

FOURTEEN

Building Community and Friendship across Difference

> We have been slowly, systematically trained by capitalism out of joining. We have been isolated … We want to have absolute control over our environments at all time, we have been taught to be rigid, we have been told that to get our own way in everything is an expression of personal power … We have been shunned out of developing emotional intelligence that allows for us to accept other foods, other music, otherness. We have been trained to conquer difference rather than join.
>
> —MOE BOWNSTERN, "Living in the Backswing"[1]

At the beginning of this book I wrote about how much it influenced my thinking on friendship when I had top surgery and felt let down by friends I had thought would be there for me. My partner at the time had also been feeling let down by her friendships, and we decided to work together on "building community" no matter how disappointed we were feeling. Our solution was to start hosting monthly potlucks, which we did for a little more than a year. The concept was to have a standing event that we could invite friends and potential friends to and to which they could also bring their own friends. People we loved would meet one another and our relationships would become more of a network, less of a series of one-on-one relationships, like I wrote about in Chapter 3. It didn't work as we thought it would though, and we ended up giving up on the potlucks. It was too disappointing how often people said they were going to come and then bailed at the last minute.

I came to realize that I'd been working on my friendships to try and solve a lack of community, but those are different things. I am fortunate to have lots of friends and to be pretty comfortable both maintaining my friendships and starting new ones. The absence I was feeling was not a lack of friendships or of time with my friends; it was community.

One of the insights that helped clarify my thinking was a thread on X from @pangmeli:

> I'm all for activist communities, queer communities etc, but communities are few and far between. what we have more of are scenes. two signs that it's a scene: it doesn't have multiple generations (children, elders) and the members all have a suspiciously similar aesthetic
>
> I think when a community or scene isn't diverse enough — and by diverse I don't just mean demographics, but also diverse walks of life, diverse ways of seeing the world, diverse levels of personal development — it becomes prone to a lot of problems. it's too clumped up[2]

Thinking about this point I realized how nebulous the concept of community is and how easy it is to use it indiscriminately, relying on it to carry weight without being clear on what you mean by it. "The queer community" can mean a demographic of people who share certain experiences but may not know or like one another, or it can mean "me and my friends." Reflecting on the distinction between a community and a scene made it clear to me that I had scenes but wanted community: relationships with people of different generations who were in many ways different from me, while sharing some core values or intentions.

The Religious Society of Friends

Around that same time I went to the baptism of an adult friend who had recently made her faith a bigger part of her life and joined a church. Seeing her surrounded by members of her religious community of a wide range of ages who were so happy for her, I realized that that was exactly what I would want for people I love, and for myself as well.

I was raised as a Quaker, in the religion that is formally known as the Religious Society of Friends (for real: no wonder I am like this). My parents were mostly secular and, as I understand it, more into Quakerism for the community and social justice aspects: my father joined after coming to Canada as a Vietnam War draft dodger. I left Quakerism when I was in my teens. After struggling to make the potlucks a thing, it occurred to me that I had essentially been trying to reverse engineer what people who regularly attend a place of worship have: a low-pressure way of getting together regularly without having to specifically organize each gathering. Inverting the more common formulation, I'd consider myself "religious but not spiritual." I neither experience presence-of-god type feelings nor feel bothered by their absence. I just like showing up to be with people. This is something generally acceptable within Quakerism, or the flavour of it that I've been around. Quakerism is nominally Christian and a lot of Quakers are Christian, but you don't have to be (I'm not).

I think that friendship, at its best, offers us glimpses of ways of liking people for reasons outside of conventionally valued attributes, like certain kinds of beauty and sexual attractiveness, wealth, and concordance with dominant values and ideals. Maybe this is because friendship flies somewhat under the radar, not policed to the same extent as romantic relationships. More space is given in friendships for appreciating people for a diversity of reasons: because they are caring, because they are funny, because you learn a lot from them. I hope that being able to value these qualities in our friends makes room in our hearts for questioning why there are so few qualities for which people are celebrated and to value more people in more ways.

Likewise, to me, community is about extending your sense of obligation beyond your curated collection of friends to other people you share space with regardless of your feelings toward them. It is about claiming people and asking to be claimed. In *On Community*, Casey Plett writes,

> My argument is that community is a vital but oft-neglected sibling of those rarefied entities that keep one away from isolation and despair; it rests right

> up there with cherished friends, a partner who loves you, a family of some stripe who love you back, a passion or commitment that gives you juice through the days. Few of us enjoy all those things in this life (I currently don't). But some combo of them makes existence worth living (as it does mine). I want to argue for community's import alongside them. I think even the most private and introverted among us still benefit deeply from community connections; almost everyone knows what it's like to enter a space with other humans and feel warmth.[3]

I don't have all those different categories of relationship either, but my life is made warmer and more meaningful by even simple and fleeting moments of convivial connection with others, whether it's chatting about the weather, waving at a baby passing in a stroller, or griping about the bus being late. Although Casey specifies "with other humans," I think that relationships with land, plants, and other-than-human beings can also provide precious warmth and belonging.

Casey resists offering a definition of community but instead glances at it from a variety of angles, although later in the book she offers the phrase "an ongoing space of encounter." And that's exactly what I had in mind when I felt weary of organizing potlucks and went back to Quakerism: something ongoing where I could be part of a rotating cast of others. I often hear people wish for a "secular version of church" or "church without religion," but I don't know if I have seen any successful attempts at bringing that about. My friend Cassey, who was raised in a mainstream Protestant church and is seeking queer and activist communities as an adult, sees some important "aspects of 'churchness' that are hard to replicate, specifically in contrast to online spaces." They offered this list of what they see as the constituents of "churchness":

- A membership structure that comes with defined responsibilities: you sign a membership card and then if you're an active member, you have various things you're supposed to do with that. For example, donate money or vote at the annual meeting.
- Mingling opportunities: zooms are uniquely bad for this, because you can't wander off to chat with another little circle of people for a few minutes when you want to during coffee hour, or overhear some other table talking about something and lean over to join in. There's too much structure around small groups, or not enough (if no breakouts at all are happening).
- Other events: chances to see people not just again and again on Sunday morning, but also at other times for other purposes: bringing sandwiches to a funeral, the potluck dinner, the softball team, bringing the kids to mid-week activities, book clubs and, knitting circles and whatever else.
- Committees for shared decision making and shared sense of ownership of what happens in the church.

- Longevity: established churches operate on the scale of years and decades; nothing online feels like it's going to last that long even if it has been around for a while. There's a richness that comes from that kind of history/the expectation of having a history that will last that long, that creates new possibilities.

Many people who have had bad experiences with religion yearn for a version of religious community that leaves out all the coercive and traumatic elements of religion. It can also be tempting to imagine having the nourishing aspects of religious community and practice in a way that we can just drop into and experience anytime on our own terms. However, Cassey's list helped clarify for me how much the good stuff comes from intertwining our lives with others even at times and in ways that are annoying and inconvenient. You might not *want* to bring sandwiches to that funeral, but if you want people to show up when you are bereaved and hungry, you have to do your part. In the *New York Times Magazine* article "Why Is the Loneliness Epidemic So Hard to Cure?" Richard Weissbourd, a psychologist who researches loneliness, speaks to the correlation between the rise of loneliness and the decline in Americans who attend religious services, describing religious communities as spaces that impart, among other things, "a sense that you have obligations to your ancestors and to your descendants."[4] It turns out that the obligation part is a load-bearing element. We cannot remove it and still expect to reap the benefits of community.

I don't believe it's the only solution, but I am using the example of religion in this chapter because it is the clearest way I know to get at what I mean. I have many friends whose religious faith and practice, across many religious traditions, is an important part of their lives, ethics, and social worlds. I also have many friends who have had terrible experiences with religion, who have experienced homophobia, transphobia, or sexual abuse at church or who struggle to find anti-Zionist Jewish community.

Coming Out into Collectivity

I wish I could tell you that there are many robust accessible alternatives to religion that provide the same good things but won't subject you to any of the bad things. Specifically, I'd really love for this to be true of queer and trans spaces. It is enticing to think that it may once have been. In *Families We Choose: Lesbians, Gays, Kinship*, which we looked at in Chapter 4, Kath Weston writes,

> During the 1970s the concept of community came to embody practical wisdom emerging from the bars, friendship networks, and a spate of new gay organizations: the knowledge that lesbians and gay men, joining together on the basis of a sexual identity, could create enduring social ties. In the process, sexuality was reconstituted as a ground of common experience rather than a quintessentially personal domain.[5]

Weston names a moment in time when there was the physical and social infrastructure — like bars and community organizations — that made it possible for queer people to gather in groups rather than just in sexual or romantic pairs. Gathering in groups caused people to think of themselves as members of a collective with common cause and responsibility to one another. These two factors — the community spaces and the community identity — reinforce one another.

This infrastructure of queer "third spaces," like bars, bookstores, and bathhouses, has suffered the same fate as many other places where people gather outside of work and home. When I look at this definition of community, I remember that "coming out" did not originally mean telling the mostly straight people in your life that you're gay, but "coming out" in the camp sense of a debutante ball: making your debut in the bars and the scene. It is hard not to think that, while more of us are "out" in the contemporary sense of openly queer, sexuality has reverted to being more of a "quintessentially personal domain," something it is possible to do alone, within only a couple or nuclear family, or primarily online.

In *Everyday Acts & Small Subversions: Women Reinventing Family, Community, and Home*, which we look at again in Chapter 15, Andee Hochman, writing in the 1990s, well before gay marriage was legal in the US, quotes Sarah Schulman: "There's this push for domestic partnership laws, for gay marriage. But if the gay community was divided up into privatized marriage family units, and wasn't a community, the response to AIDS would never have been what it has been."[6]

I think this is an interesting argument against gay marriage. The arguments I am accustomed to hearing are, first, that it was unconscionable to devote resources to an issue that would only benefit the most privileged members of a largely broke and struggling demographic, and second, that it points us toward heterosexual norms rather than embracing our freak shit. Schulman's argument could be seen as a variation on that second point, but I think it's fascinating to consider the ways in which the availability of marriage points us away from community. When a normative flavour of coupledom is available, we are less likely to throw in our lot with the motley collection we know from the bars, whom we may dislike but who are nevertheless part of the same collectivity. We get pickier with our time and care. I am trying to undo that shift within my own life and heart and to always be broadening the scope of who I care about and for.

It's not easy to swim against the tide of narrowing down the scope of your life and care. But it feels great to be part of a broader collectivity. If you have been in queer or activist spaces, you have probably felt the misery of feeling a group winnow itself down to the True Believers. Sometimes, groups land on too narrow a range of permitted ideas, tactics, or vocabulary and make it clear, explicitly or implicitly, that you cannot organize with them unless you are on the same page. We need some amount of consensus or alignment to get things done, but I see a lot of benefit in working with a diversity of tactics toward a common goal or organizing with people who share common experiences even if we use different words to describe them. I'm open to being challenged and held accountable, but being held to a narrow consensus feels bad. In organizing, in friendship, in spaces of community gathering, we need more ability to live with difference than what I have experienced.

The concept of community gets at a sense of interconnectedness, whether ambient or intentional, in our lives. And I suspect that the reason the concept of community is so hard to put a finger on has to do with how much our interconnectedness, for many of us, has rotted out, if it was ever present at all. Community is, was, could be a domain of care other than friendship, other than romantic and familial love, other than what we can buy on the private market, if we can afford it.

When I moved back to Montreal, I started attending Quaker meeting again. I was thrilled when, soon afterwards, the meeting decided to start a Committee of Care to facilitate collective responses to participants' needs for material and emotional support. I feel deeply grateful to be able to improve my capacity for care and mutual aid from people with a lot of experience and sensitivity in that domain and to know that it will be there for me when I am the person in need. Religious or ritual practice can be a strong way of binding people together to care for one another, although its bonds can also turn coercive and cruel. In Chapter 15, we look at the role ritual can play in deepening and strengthening friendships.

FIFTEEN

Returning to Ritual, Celebration, and Grief

> [We are] losing the power of celebration. Instead of celebrating, [we seek] to be amused or entertained. Celebration is an active state, an act of expressing reverence or appreciation. To be entertained is a passive state — it is to receive pleasure afforded by an amusing act or a spectacle. Celebration is a confrontation, giving attention to the transcendent meaning of one's actions.
>
> —ABRAHAM JOSHUA HESCHEL, *Who Is Man*[1]

In 2008 I was finishing an undergraduate degree in philosophy at McGill University. I was writing a thesis on the philosophy of music and working as an assistant to the wonderfully kind Professor Eric Lewis, who taught mostly Pre-Socratic philosophy but also moonlighted as a trumpet player in Montreal's free improv jazz scene. At a conference I helped organize on the philosophy of improvised music, we had a workshop with the inimitable experimental composer Pauline Oliveros. Snowed in at her home in upstate New York, she ended up presenting over video conference (still a novelty back then). She led us through an exercise where all of us were asked to move slowly around the room in whatever paths we each chose, singing a song that was meaningful to us as slowly as we possibly could.

It was almost impossible to hear what anyone else was singing. I was grateful for that because I'd chosen the overly revealing Carter Family song "Will the Circle Be Unbroken," which is about the feeling of having everything you thought you knew being called into question by the force of grief. I walked aimlessly through the room singing my sad song slowly, everyone else unintelligibly singing on their own paths, and the sounds of our voices converged around one droning pitch, all the melodies woven together. Later, in the Q&A part of the presentation, someone asked Oliveros about this and she brushed it off impatiently, saying, "Yes, everyone found the resonant frequency of the room and stayed there; that's what usually happens." All rooms have frequencies or pitches that ring out more loudly than others, depending on complicated interactions between sound waves and the size and shape of the room. Although it was banal for Pauline Oliveros, I've thought about it from time to time ever since. That a room full of people, some of whom were musicians or especially avid listeners, some of whom were total civilians like me, could with our untrained voices limn a hidden quality of a physical space and collectively form an unspoken agreement to stay there together seemed strange and beautiful.

I was remembering this again recently in Quaker meeting for worship. Quakers believe that there is an "inner light" or "that of god" in everyone. Quaker religious gatherings don't have a pastor or a sermon: people sit in a circle together in silence and anyone who feels "moved by the spirit" may speak briefly to the group. People share memories, observations, preoccupations, songs. Whether the words someone shares seem profound or misguided or confusing or wise to you, you receive them in silence. Sometimes nobody speaks at all. In the absence of an activity and usually in the absence of much speaking or movement, I have the strong sense of just being a person sharing space with other people. Sometimes it feels like we are tending to or casting our collective regard on something; sometimes it feels as though we are labouring through or struggling at something together. Sometimes it feels like that Pauline Oliveros workshop where we are all drifting around each other, both feeling out and building some invisible sense of collectivity. Sometimes it doesn't feel like anything other than sitting around waiting for the hour to end, but that's OK too. The concept of "holding space" often feels meaningless and cliché, but in meeting for worship, whether I'm personally feeling it that week, I still feel like I am holding space in an almost literal way, like I can be a load-bearing element of the collective just by being there.

When I first started going back to Quaker meeting as an adult I was worried about my ability to sit in silence, alone with my thoughts, for an hour at a time, but there's something about doing it in the presence of other people that makes it manageable for me even when I feel anxious or emotional. Hearing other people sigh, stretch, or even fall asleep and snore, helps me regulate my own breathing and body. I find it intimate and warm. If you aren't up on psychology jargon, "co-regulation" is when two or more people emotionally regulate together, allowing one or more of them to return to a state of calm that would have been harder for them to access on their own. We begin as infants to learn this skill from our caregivers: to slow our breathing and heart rate in tune with another's, to borrow and learn from someone else's ability to be present and feel safe.

When we sing or chant or recite together it can align our breathing and our mood to one another's. In this, religious observances can be powerful spaces of co-regulation. Quaker meeting has taught me that this can also happen by sharing silent space together in an intentional way. At their best, religious spaces offer us co-regulation along with opportunities to look out for and care for one another, to eat together, to build a consensus on ethics and values and act on them. In short, religion can provide not only opportunities to connect but the actual ability to connect with others — to find the resonant frequency of a room, if you will.

Many of the worst atrocities I know of, from world-historical events to individual abuses, have been, are currently being, and will be carried out in the name of religion. Some of the people closest to me have experienced such awful violence, cruelty, and mistreatment in religious spaces and communities that they are unlikely to ever experience religion as a place of safety and care. I would never say that religion is a straightforwardly good thing any more than I would say family is, or friendship for that matter. But I do think collective ritual is important. Religion is a major type of collective ritual but far from the only one. I experience a sense of togetherness and collective regulation at Quaker meeting; I also experience it when I am at a protest marching in the streets with hundreds of others. One of my favourite chants is "If we don't get it, shut it down! Shut it down, shut it down!" The "shut it downs" get louder and faster, and as they do I never fail to feel a joy and rage that's bigger than myself, shared across the body of the march.

Invitation into Ritual

An invitation into a ritual or ceremony always feels to me like the greatest possible gift. In 2017 Canada was celebrating the 150th anniversary of its confederation. On June 28, a few days before Canada Day was to be celebrated on July 1, the Bawaating Water Protectors set up a tipi on a ragged sloping edge of Parliament Hill, the seat of Canada's colonial government, and a few blocks from where I lived at the time. In the dark they wrested tipi poles away from police and managed to erect the structure. The next day they announced that they planned to move the tipi from this out-of-the-way corner up onto higher ground into the midst of the parcel of unceded Algonquin territory that was currently being set up for a huge noisy celebration of the 150th anniversary of Canada's founding. They called for settlers to come help by acting as a buffer against the police, to come listen, to bring dry socks and cell phone battery packs.

In the driving rain we took the tipi down. We unwrapped the canvas from the poles and disengaged the poles one by one from the tipi, placing them across the shoulders of a group of people who stood ready to carry them in a bundle to the new location. My friend Liam and I stepped forward to lift one of the poles, and someone shouted instructions to us: wait, bring it this way, don't let it touch the ground once you've lifted it, OK, now bring it here. It was an immense honour to take part in this as a white settler on unceded land. That day, a particular place was given to us specifically as settlers to witness this ceremony and to assist in certain ways. I was grateful to be asked to help and that the ways it was and was not appropriate for me to take part were spelled out explicitly.

The group of people carrying the poles moved slowly down the street and back through the Parliament gates with the rest of us alongside, with the Canada150 sound and light show cranking into gear, lighting the rain up purple and neon. We were soaked through raincoats and up sleeves, umbrellas sending sluices of water down the shoulders of our neighbours when we didn't watch closely. And my heart was full. Making that request of settlers during our crass and tacky celebration of conquest took work, care, empathy, and trust.

To receive care, you generally need to be able to ask. You need the ability to trust or reasonably hope that the request will be well met, which is hard because we've all been burned before. It is difficult to ask for care when your needs are desperate, perilous, high stakes, when you're surviving on scraps, adrenaline, spite, and hope. Ritual can provide a space where we can access a depth of shared feeling without necessarily having to disclose the particulars of our lives and without having to know whether we agree on everything. Sometimes I feel like the options for friendships are either surface-level catch-ups over coffee or trauma-bonding over miseries and sorrows. It's not that talking about hardships isn't important, but it's not the only way to go deeper in your friendships. Ritual provides a container into which the ragged, needy, seeking parts of ourselves can be poured along with our strength and capacity for joy and care.

DIY Ritual

One of the most delightful discoveries in the boatload of books on friendship I read as I wrote this book was Andee Hochman's *Everyday Acts & Small Subversions: Women Reinventing Family, Community, and Home*, from 1994. This sadly now out-of-print book is a series of vignettes profiling people in Hochman's life — mostly fellow lesbians — who had opted to set up their lives in ways outside the norm of the heterosexual monogamous suburban nuclear family and the joys and struggles they encountered in so doing.

One of the things that most struck and charmed me about the book was how many of the women describe forging new rituals for themselves when they realized that, whether by choice or by exclusion, they would not be taking part in many of the rituals that were expected of them. The book describes croning ceremonies, where her friends celebrated entering menopause and becoming elders.[2] It recounts a Change Dance, which another friend held to mark her hysterectomy, with a pile of props and costumes for every attendee to create a performance piece about an important change in her life, which included divorce, health struggles, and the death of a parent.[3] It also shares many stories of people taking existing rituals: shabbat, solstice, weddings, memorials, Hallowe'en — and making them their own. She describes a winter solstice ritual where everyone spoke of a time in their lives when they were afraid of the dark, then of "a time when you loved the dark, felt at home with it." People described "camping trips and nights clotted with stars," and Hochman recounted "sleeping on the floor of a half-built cabin in northern California, looking up through open rafters at satin-black wedges of sky."[4] It sounds like such a beautiful and meaningful way to mark the inflection point of a season.

Reading about people's self-created rituals in breadth and volume, I started to see themes and ingredients emerge. Food. Music. A host doing work ahead of time to set up an order of ceremony that nonetheless includes space for everyone to contribute and make it their own. When I think what it would take for a friendship to take on the emotional gravitas of a familial or romantic relationship, ritual comes to mind as a way to create space for emotional depth and to create a possibility or promise of recurrence and commitment across time.

This chapter was a hard one for me to write because ritual and ceremony are not a huge part of my life, although I find them compelling. I'm someone who grew up from an angry sneering atheist teenager to an earnest, sincere adult, but I still struggle to get over my own self-consciousness. Marking an occasion with a ceremony or ritual says to yourself and others "This is important to me," and it is dangerous to admit that something is important to you. It's easier to leave it unsaid: that way nobody can laugh at you or disappoint you by blowing off your invitation. I guess it's another demonstration that, regrettably, nothing really good happens without making yourself vulnerable. Trust me, I wish it weren't so. I tend to play things closer to my chest, and I let important moments of transition slide by without necessarily admitting how much they mean to me and without knowing how to invite other people into them with me. But it always feels better when I mark the big changes in my life.

Something like the Change Dance is admittedly advanced: if I was at a function and the host told me I had to prepare a fifteen-minute costumed interpretive dance about a major change in my life, I would want to excuse myself to the bathroom and crawl out the window, never to be seen again. But wouldn't it be better to be someone who could lean into that, who had the strength to be silly and vulnerable in front of their friends? To be game to do an impromptu performance about something close to your heart, and in so doing, gain access to your friend's silly and vulnerable moments too?

If you're scared like I am and not in the habit of that kind of extravagant baring of your heart, there are much easier ways of inviting others to help you mark a big change in your life. I think back warmly on the time I was moving out of a city and realizing that I hadn't done any of the big tourist things you don't tend to do in the place where you live. So I made a list of them and circulated it amongst my friends, and people joined me at various museums and overpriced tourist restaurants. It was a wonderful way to say goodbye to a place and the people I loved there.

I am grateful every time someone invites me into a container of ritual they have built. The quotation that opens this chapter was part of the haggadah my friend Julia used at her seder this year. While I'm not Jewish, I find Passover a deeply meaningful holiday that I am always happy to be able to share with my friends. Eating and telling stories together and recommitting ourselves to fighting injustice wherever and however it appears is right up my alley. Yearly holidays place a bookmark in the year, a point we can cycle back to over and over. The list of atrocities we mourn during the seder and commit to standing in the way of changes. Partners come and go, kids get bigger, we get more grey hairs and finish the night earlier. Eventually people who were around the table with us this year will die and be mourned and remembered. The yearly ritual connects us back to past versions of ourselves and to ancestors who have gone before. Repetition invokes continuity with the past and into the future, inviting us to mourn and to hope.

HOW DO YOU INCORPORATE RITUAL INTO YOUR FRIENDSHIPS?

Back in the 1980s, a group of us who read tarot got together and created an online group. Over the years people dropped out, or died, and now there are just four of us left. I consider the other three very close friends. We bonded over doing tarot readings for each other (even when the group was larger), and tarot requires a certain amount of ritual. Sometimes it is as simple as pulling out a tarot deck, thinking about the question, asking for answers, and reading the cards. Some us of talk with our "guides," which may be angels, or imaginary friends, or people we think of as being in the spirit world, or even some deeper part of our own mind. Candles may be lit, and sometimes incense.

Even a small ritual requires disconnecting from the "noise" of the obvious world, and you go to what feels like an "enclosed space" to connect with forces that feel larger and more wise. Something about ritual with someone else makes a deeper connection, deeper than it would be in everyday life. On a daily basis, we often put on "faces" with other people that fit the occasion. I'm not pretending to be someone else, but I'm not revealing the true Me either. Ritual tends to dispense with the "faces," and you meet the real person. And there is trust involved, when you make yourself that open. Knowing you can trust makes for deeper friendships. I can think of only one other friendship I have that didn't involve a ritual of some sort.

—JUDITH

I grew up in the (US) midwest in a very small, very religious town. As an undiagnosed autistic person, one aspect of religion that I was drawn to was the degree of ritual and structure. These rituals could include group fasting and related ceremonies (e.g., breaking the fast) or observations for Christmas, Easter, etc. Church services themselves were also very structured: even if we switched between churches, the general format or structure of the service would usually remain mostly the same and there was a familiarity to the hymns, benedictions, etc. In short, it made it easy to know what to expect. I think for some autistic people, it was also one environment where there could be some sense of social inclusion because the rules are so prescribed — at times in a very literal way, where there would be a script for what the pastor says and how the congregation responds. So while I didn't truly fit in, it was a way to mask some of the isolation.

I am no longer in the church, but ritual is a part of my social life in other ways. Almost all of my friends are also autistic, and we tend to find ritual and routine in our friendships. With one friend, we meet at the same time virtually every week, for the same duration and tend to follow a very routine conversational structure. Another friend and I end each of our text conversation by sending each other a picture of a chicken. For other people who are more spontaneous, that might feel confining or too rigid, but for us, it's helpful. It provides a sense of stability.

—SAM

In the early weeks of healing and recovering from Hurricane Helene, some of us began a book club to talk about those shared experiences of community that felt powerful, potent, and life-changing to us during that disaster.

The reading group was — and continues to be — open to anyone, and all types of people show up. There are regulars, and those who only come once or twice, yet typically about twenty-five people circle up in the public space of Firestorm, a queer, feminist, and anarchist bookstore in Asheville, North Carolina.

The book club is still meeting over eight months later. We've gathered in the midst of rising fascism, continued genocide, local wildfires due to governmental neglect, and deep personal loss. We are still here.

Each time we come together, we engage in what's become our own ritual in the wake of mass devastation. We put our feet on the ground and close our eyes. With N-95 masks on and each at our own pace, in the centring of a single moment, we take three deep breaths. When we have each finished and feel ready to face the group again from the interiority of our own space, we raise a hand and look into the faces of our comrades.

Many of us lost community in the days of Helene, some of us found it, and all of us lost things unforeseen in the months following. But each time we meet, we take those breaths and look into each others' faces. We know that we are here, we survived, and we are still in the absolute terror and undeniable gift of life.

— LAUREN MILLER

from the zine *Ritual as Resistance*[1]

SIXTEEN

Imagining a New World as This One Crumbles

In the dark times
Will there also be singing?
Yes, there will also be singing.
About the dark times.

—BERTOLD BRECHT, "Motto"[1]

There is an anarchist tradition here in Montreal of bussing out to a large cluster of prisons and detention centres in the suburbs on New Years' Eve and lighting fireworks and playing music over the walls. The event has given me some of the purest joy and sense of possibility that I have felt. I find it a profoundly meaningful opportunity to imagine a better world and what the process of getting there will look and feel like.

On one such night, as music played from several loudspeakers and a motley variety of musical instruments, and as we shot fireworks over prison walls, I wished we could do this every night. And it led me to imagine, as I'm sure was intended, what would happen if there were ten or a hundred or a thousand times as many of us and if we didn't stop at the gates. As we danced in the street outside a minimum-security facility, people inside came to their windows and danced with us, doing goofy synchronized dances and making hearts with their hands. One old man played the accordion at his window.

It offered the precious reminder that incarcerated people were *right there* but unable to come with us and that they were not abstractions but real, silly, joyful people who we have a moral obligation to support and to free. This is what I know and believe all the time, but nourishing that belief with lived experience of connection is vital. "We come here every year," someone shouted through a megaphone, "and we'll keep doing it forever!" To keep going we need to keep feeding each other little tastes of the world to come.

Surviving the End of the World

Perhaps people in every time and place think they're living in a moment of particular change and collapse. To some extent that's probably just what it feels like to be alive for more than a little while, to see things that were commonplace slough off and strange new things grow in their place. But many people throughout history have lived through the literal end of the world as they knew it. The Choctaw author Steven Charleston wrote *We Survived the End of the World: Lessons from Native America on Apocalypse and Hope* about the experience of belonging to a culture that has already survived multiple apocalypses. His ancestors survived the Trail of Tears, a forced displacement hundreds of miles to the west of their homelands. Thousands of their friends, family, and neighbours did not survive. Charleston points out that the feeling many people have now, especially people whose ancestors have not faced genocide in living memory, as we contemplate how climate collapse and rising fascism will change our lives beyond recognition and that many of us will live shorter and more painful lives than we would like, is nothing new.[2] This isn't to say it doesn't matter — nothing could possibly matter more — or that we should give up — I feel strongly we should all fight with everything we have — but that there exists guidance for this moment.

In his 2018 paper "Deep Adaptation: A Map for Navigating Climate Tragedy," UK professor Jem Bendell defines societal collapse as "an uneven ending of our normal modes of sustenance, shelter, security, pleasure, identity and meaning," specifying,

> when I say starvation, destruction, migration, disease and war, I mean in your own life. With the power down, soon you wouldn't have water coming out of your tap. You will depend on your neighbours for food and some warmth. You will become malnourished. You won't know whether to stay or go. You will fear being violently killed before starving to death.[3]

If you and the people close to you haven't experienced starvation, war, and losing access to things like water and electricity for long periods of time, as I haven't, it is easy to think of these as things that happen elsewhere, to other people. I am sure everyone feels the same way until it happens to them. Along similar lines, the American climate activist Bill McKibben writes,

> We've come through 75 years where having neighbors was essentially optional: if you had a credit card, you could get everything you needed to survive dropped off at your front door. But the next 75 years aren't going to be like that; we're going to need to return to the basic human experience of relying on the people around you. We're going to need to rediscover that we're a social species, which for Americans will be hard.[4]

The scale of the changes that need to happen for our world to be a liveable one are immense. But they are also an accretion of infinitely many small changes that lead us back in the direction of what McKibben calls rediscovering ourselves as a social species. When we no longer have the option of ordering anything we need online and having a stranger deliver it to our door within 48 hours, when the medications we rely on stop being readily available, when supermarket shelves are empty, we will need to ask one another for help, and we are going to have to figure it out together.

Bendell also writes in "Deep Adaptation" that he has found that embracing hopelessness can also make room for action. When people are able to contemplate social collapse "in a supportive environment, where we have enjoyed community with each other, celebrating ancestors and enjoying nature before then looking at this information and possible framings for it, something positive happens," and people tend to begin to envision what new possibilities might rise from the ashes of the old.

My own inclination is always to seek safety in separation and independence, in making sure I have what I need. As mentioned before, I always have food stashed in my room and in my backpack in case I need to hide or bolt. A sense of danger or scarcity will push you toward whatever feels safest for you. If you are like me, self-reliance might feel most safe. But as we've seen, there is no such thing: even if you're living alone in a hut you built in the forest, you are reliant on and in a relationship with other living things. If your self-reliance consists of a bunch of MREs you bought online, those were made by and brought to your door by other people. Neither of those types of self-reliance is likely to be your best bet for surviving the collapse of your way of life. Individualism might feel safest, but it almost certainly isn't. If we want to get through this — for pretty much any value of "this" — we need to rewire ourselves to orient toward connection instead of isolation. With every loving bond we forge, we divorce ourselves a little more from the demons that haunt us — hopelessness, irony, and complacency — and find sparks of possibility. We have to try and fail and try again and again to connect with one another, through frustration and disappointment and loss.

The Friendship Hospital

In the first year or so of the COVID-19 pandemic, I had a recurring fantasy. Like many people I was desperately lonely. Sometimes I was lonely to an extent that it started to seem like an emergency. I would think, this might be a mental health crisis, maybe I should go to the hospital. But I know what the psych ward can offer, and it wasn't anything I needed or wanted in that moment. Instead, I envisioned what I called the Friendship Hospital. I haven't told anyone about this fantasy until now. I vividly and desperately imagined being able to go somewhere soft and warm, be held and have someone run their fingers through my hair, talk and laugh with me, share food, help me out with whatever I needed help with. The Friendship Hospital would be open to everyone at all times, and the care dispensed there would be given with complete sincerity. These were all types of care I desired, but the fantasy was specifically of them being made available universally to all. This is not what a regular hospital is like, something that would be emphasized to me later when I was keeping my friend company in one, as I write about in the introduction to Part 2.

In her essay "Did Your Utopia Already Exist?" Elise Granata describes the experience of looking through old newsletters at the Lesbian Herstory Archives and realizing that her home state of Connecticut, while not home to any storied queer metropoles like New York or San Francisco, had nevertheless had a thriving lesbian feminist social infrastructure in the 1970s and 80s, with "multi-floor gathering centers and Women's Liberation Rock Bands and clubs and meeting spaces and venues ... And all the little gatherings in between: potlucks, meet-ups, talking circles, book clubs, classes. And the SERVICES: credit unions, childcare, divorce advice, job centers, political alliances and unions."[5] Marvelling at this rich ecosystem, this whole alternative social world, she asks that we "let these histories be a reminder: it isn't so wild to want the spaces, experiences, and social infrastructure of our dreams. We have decades of wisdom to look back on, to learn from, to riff on and make better."

I am obsessed with radical histories because the easiest way to know what is possible is to learn what has already existed. While I wrote this book, I read about different ways that people have arranged their social lives and the social infrastructure of their lives. I read about communes, cohousing, and co-ops, mutual aid projects, the community-run "health clinics, food centres, kitchens and legal aid hubs"[6] that popped up all over Greece during and since its austerity crisis, and peer respite houses where people can get help with their substance use with support from other people with experience of addiction. I read about the Black Panthers' social programs, like their famous free breakfasts, which shamed school systems into offering kids breakfast lest they cede moral ground to Black radicals. I read about all these things as I was trying to write about friendship. I kept stopping myself and thinking, OK, but a free health clinic isn't friendship. Why does this feel relevant?

It feels relevant because the more I've thought and written and talked about friendship and about how to transform our friendships so that they can meet the need for the community, chosen family, and radical care that I keep talking about wanting, the more I have realized how much I need to change about my life. All these examples are, in some way, a Friendship Hospital where types of care are offered up more broadly and generously than what is usual under capitalism, outside of the profit motive or the strictures of the couple or nuclear family.

A lot of us have at least some sense of what the relationships we desire look like, even as they slip from our grasp or get crushed to gunk in our fists. The more I thought about it the more I realized the question was: What would the world need to look like, in concrete and specific terms, for us to be able to have the types of friendships we yearn for? It is harder to build and imagine than to critique, but as Robyn Maynard and Leanne Betasamosake Simpson put it, "It is never enough to just critique the system and name our oppression. We also have to create the alternative, on the ground and in real time."[7] Similarly, in her book *Hope in the Dark*, Rebecca Solnit describes the politics of prefiguration, "the idea that if you embody what you aspire to, you have already succeeded."[8]

This life is short, short, short. As the years of your life accrue, the endings and losses pile up. People die, or they fuck off, or you fall out of touch. The result for me has been a greater sense of urgency each year of my life to try and live right: do right by the people in my life, maintain a desperate curiosity about everyone, make art and make it easier for other people to make art. This immediacy and urgency are the essence of prefigurative politics. It's also a sensible approach to a world suffering climate collapse. As an upper-middle-class kid in the 1990s I saw my dad planning for the retirement he's now enjoying in the 2020s, and I was led to believe that if I too worked desk jobs for a couple decades, maybe I could spend my elder years travelling and enjoying hobbies and friendship. I don't think it's going to work out that way. First of all, I turned out to be too crazy for a full-time job; second, pensions are rapidly eroding as a feature of even middle-class life; and third, what will the world be like in 2051 when I'm 65? Almost certainly not a place of stability and ease. I've realized I'd probably better take moments and months of retirement wherever I can get them. Anything that it is important to me to do within my life I should do whenever I have the chance. It is desperately urgent to me to live out my values right now and as deeply as possible.

In Chapter 7, I wrote about how having cheap Manhattan rent throughout the middle of the 20th century allowed Samuel Delany to be an artist and a freak and a maker of freaky art. In his book *Times Square Red, Times Square Blue*, Delany is explicit and thoughtful about the larger economic forces that made his social life possible. The book made me consider care as a function of breadth — belonging to a larger social fabric — as well as depth. He writes about sex with men of a wide range of ages, identities, appearances, and class and racial backgrounds, and with men who were homeless, who were recently out of psychiatric hospitals, with men he later learned died of AIDS or froze to death on the street. He suggests that "given the mode of capitalism under which we live, life is at its most rewarding, productive, and pleasant when large numbers of people understand, appreciate, and seek out interclass contact and communication conducted in a mode of good will." Delany writes about sometimes helping men out with food or cash, but their encounters aren't based around charity, but in a reciprocal intimacy. I don't have many (any?) spaces in my life where I interact intimately, which isn't to say necessarily sexually, with a range of folks whose identities and backgrounds differ massively from my own. But *Times Square Red, Times Square Blue* makes a strong case for the importance of care and intimacy not just in our closest relationships but in the more tenuous or circumstantial ones as well. He writes that these relationships "braided. They interwove. They were simultaneous … [They] did not annoy or in any way distress the man I was living with at the time — because they had their limits. They were not the central relationships of my life. They made that central relationship richer, however, by relieving it of many anxieties."[9]

Even if you, like Delany, are fortunate enough to have a big close relationship at the centre of your life, with someone on whom you can rely for intimacy, care, company and day-to-day support, you can still benefit from "encounters," friends, roommates, acquaintances, lovers, hookups, and all the many ways we have of building and maintaining ties to one another to share this world as we reach for the world to come.

How Do We Get Back Our Joy?

I deeply believe there is still a lot of joy to be had no matter how cruel the world gets, and it is getting very cruel indeed. But I believe equally strongly that to get your hands on it, you do need to be bold and insistent, like the Lucinda Williams song I mentioned in this book's preface. You need to consider what your values actually are and then move them as close to the centre of your life as you can. Like Annie Dillard wrote, "How we spend our days is, of course, how we spend our lives."[10] I have realized many times over that how I am spending my days is not how I wish to be spending my life. I am continuously trying to adjust course to balance the necessity of survival with the necessity of joy and meaning-making. In my case, this has meant opening myself up for friendship to occupy a more expansive and meaningful terrain than it is usually afforded.

In the years to come, one of the few things that seems like a relatively safe prediction is that we will need one another more than ever. Friendship can't solve all the world's ills but it can help with some of them, and our choice is probably to suffer alone or to suffer together. We can chip away at the calcified loneliness of our lives, divest from isolation, and invest in friendship. We can shift one tiny aspect of our lives at a time: from isolation to connection, from buying to borrowing, from hoarding to lending, from lending to forgetting whose it even was to start with or why that mattered. We can braid, and interweave, and we can relinquish convenience in favour of the astonishing, annoying joy of being in the world.

Acknowledgements

I write about something when I can't stop thinking about it and want to clarify and organize my thoughts, to get them out of my head and into the world. Writing is also, for me, prefigurative: it's a means by which I set an intention and lay out the way I wish to think and act and be. This project gave me a reason to go deep in conversations with friends I already knew and to make new connections with other people who are interested in thinking deeply about friendship and placing it closer to the centre of their lives. I have found having big projects and themes in my life a boon to my friendships. For the past many years, these have been zines and friendship for me. I am deeply grateful to the world of zines and zine making for providing me with a method to think through ideas in community.

My father, John, and my sibling, Clare, have encouraged and supported my writing for almost 40 years: thank you both. My mother, Susan, died when I was a kid but was by all accounts a wonderful friend.

I am grateful for the people who generously spoke to me for this book, including Andi, Calev, Cara, Cassey, Erin, Hannah, Hingman, Imogen, India, Judith, Julia, Julie, Kat, Kate, Khameleon, Mariah, Marlaina, Meghan, Mina, Ocean, Sam, Tim, Willy, and Veronika. Special thanks to Twoey Gray, my Asexuality Consultant.

I am especially grateful to my friend River Halen, who has been extremely generous in sharing their own experiences, talking through the ideas in this book, and giving vital insight into many aspects of the process of bringing a book into the world. Jeff Miller also provided invaluable support, resources, and cheerleading. I am grateful for the two writing groups in whose company I wrote much of this book, the Dick's Lending Library writing group and Metonymy Press' Unruly Writers group. Living with Corie Waugh, one of the best roommates imaginable, has also gone a long way to making this book and every other good thing in my life possible.

I would like to thank the people who helped bring this book into the world via Fernwood Publishing: the book was edited incisively and compassionately by Fazeela Jiwa; Lauren Jeanneau and Rebecca Poulin made the book beautiful. Thank you as well to Anumeha Gokhale for coordinating marketing, Art Bouman for publicity support, and Brenda Conroy for copyediting. If this book is in your hands, it's because of the good work of these excellent people.

I am also grateful to John Samson Fellows for giving his blessing for me to quote the lyrics to "(Hospital Vespers)" in this book's title.

Of course, I want to thank all the friends who are still in my life, but also those who are no longer in my life through drift, changes in circumstances, death, or irreparable conflict. In writing this book, some of the friendships that were foremost in my mind were ones that have ended. Maybe having seen their full arc makes them easier to think through than the friendships in my life that are still alive and changing. Maybe they have third acts that are still to come. In any case, I am grateful.

Glossary

affinity group: An autonomous group of people acting toward a shared goal, outside of government or commercial structures.

allosexual: Someone who experiences normative sexual attraction, in contrast to an asexual person.

alloromantic: Someone who experiences normative romantic attraction, in contrast to an aromantic person.

amatonormativity: Treating romantic relationships as though they are more important than all others, whether on a personal level or formally through structures like laws and policies.

asexual: Someone who experiences little to no sexual attraction, in contrast to an allosexual person. Definitions vary within the community, but what is often shared is a non-normative relationship to dominant cultural expectations of sex, sexuality, and sexual desire.

aromantic: Someone who experiences little to no romantic attraction, in contrast to an alloromantic person, although as with asexuality, aromanticism encompasses a broad range of non-normative relationships with romance and dating.

bottomlining: Guaranteeing that a project will be completed, or a need fulfilled, no matter what, whether you do it yourself or arrange for someone else to do it.

chosen family: People you claim as family but don't have blood or legal ties with, usually friends with a strong mutual expectation of commitment to and material support of one another.

community: A group of people, whether strictly or loosely defined, who share a space and resources and who therefore need to figure out amongst themselves things like standards and norms of behaviour, shared vocabulary, and ways of resolving differences.

community preparedness: Preparing for adverse events like natural disasters with an emphasis on sharing resources and working collaboratively toward the well-being of all, rather than expecting individuals and families to fend for themselves.

deep adaptation: The concept, as articulated by Jem Bendell, that we need to prepare both logistically and emotionally for the effects of climate change to disrupt the infrastructure of industrialized society to the extent of causing widespread social collapse, including in wealthier parts of the world that consider themselves insulated from extreme climate events and attending social disruption.

kin: Family, often used in a way that is more expansive than blood and legal family but still holding a meaningful sense of obligation. As Patty Krawec points out in *Becoming Kin*, kinship relations may also be specific and carry particular obligations, such as how being an aunt or uncle is different from being a niece/nephew/nibling, or from being a parent.[1]

mutual aid: A term for when people help each other meet their material needs in a way that may be more or less formally organized, but that crucially is non-hierarchical and flows in multiple directions rather than being a relationship where one group helps and the other is helped.

neoliberalism: An ideology and set of political and economic policies where people are expected to be fundamentally self-reliant, rather than interdependent, and that accordingly demolishes social services, community organizations, and social safety nets.

One Dish, One Spoon treaty: An agreement to share land peacefully in a spirit of mutual co-operation, originating in Haudenosaunee and Anishinaabeg traditions.

public affluence: Investing in making shared high-quality resources broadly available, as opposed to hoarding them for the use of an individual, family, or small in-group.

prefiguration: Bringing about the world you desire by acting as though you already live in that world, even if only in a partial and temporary way.

Quakerism: An offshoot of Protestant Christianity formally known as the Religious Society of Friends, some of whose members worship in silence, with anyone present welcome to minister, rather than having a designated clergy. Many North American Quakers also have strong ties to civil rights, social justice, and peace movements.

queerplatonic: A relationship that is committed and intimate and may occupy a role in someone's life similar to a conventional romantic partnership but is not romantic and challenges the notion that the central relationship in one's life is assumed to be a romantic connection.

social safety net: A structure for making sure everyone's needs get met on a broader scale than families, friendships, or other forms of individual-level social ties and not dependent on someone's material resources or relationships.

WASP: "White Anglo-Saxon Protestant." A term used in the United States, Canada, and some other former colonies of England to refer to people of the background described, with an implication that they skew toward being wealthy, emotionally repressed, and valuing propriety over honesty, vulnerability, and justice.

zine: A self-published, free or cheap, consciously unprofessional and imperfect publication, circulated within a subculture or social circle with an expectation of reciprocity, with lineages in punk, fandom, resistance movements, and/or underground art, depending on who you ask.

Summaries, Discussion Questions, and Actions

1 | Do We Even Know What Friendship Is?

Compared to romantic or family relationships, friendship is a broad and ambiguous category. It encompasses a wide range of connections that vary in form, depth, intimacy, duration, and expectations. While this flexibility can be liberating and can allow friendships to shift and endure over time, it can also result in hurtful mismatches in expectation.

Question: If there are friendships in your life that you feel dissatisfied with, how do you think they would they need to change to work better?

Action: Think of two friendships you have or have had in the past. How were they different from one another in terms of factors like the amount of time you spent together, the activities you shared, and the amount of emotional vulnerability in the relationship? Are you drawn to one particular format for your friendships, or do they tend to look different from one another?

2 | Casual Sex, Serious Friendships, and Life Outside the Couple

Asexual thinkers highlight how intimacy, passion, and commitment can exist in relationships that are not necessarily romantic or sexual. Conversely, sexual relationships can also hold deep care and trust without necessarily being romantic. In practice, we can combine friendship, sex, romance, commitment, and other components of relationships however we want, but doing so in non-normative ways can be difficult. Ultimately, friendship's ambiguity makes it both liberating and precarious when it's taken seriously as an important relationship.

Question: What do you think moves a relationship outside of the realm of friendship? Sex? Certain types of feelings? Where do you think your personal definition of the boundaries of friendship come from?

Action: Think of a friend who you feel you do, or could, share a sense of mutual commitment with, and have a conversation with them about your friendship and your commitment to it and each other.

3 | Weaving Networks of Friendship

Friendship is often defined as a relationship between two individuals, but friendships are both more fun and more resilient when they take place within a network of connections. Concentrating too much responsibility in a single relationship, whether romantic or platonic, breeds strain and disappointment and allows abuse to fester. By contrast, friendships embedded in broader networks allow for collective problem-solving and greater accountability.

Question: When has one of your one-on-one relationships benefitted from the insight of a third person?

Action: Think of some friends you have who don't already know each other but who you think might enjoy each other's company, and ask them if they'd like to be introduced to each other.

4 | The Families We Choose

Queer people and communities often place extraordinary weight on friendship and "chosen family." The concept has roots in Black, racialized, and working-class communities where kinship beyond blood has long been material, political, and necessary but has become abstracted and idealized as it travelled into whiter, more middle-class queer circles. Chosen family often functions as an ideal of lasting, non-hierarchical intimacy, even among those of us who don't necessarily have the skills to fully enact it.

Question: When you were growing up, were there a lot of other adults around helping each other out and keeping each other company, or mostly just your immediate family? How did those experiences shape the way you've set up your own life?

Action: Find someone who grew up in a different configuration than you did: someone who grew up with mostly just a nuclear family unit if you grew up with a big extended family, friends, and community around, or vice versa. Talk about what you each loved and found frustrating about those ways of setting up a life.

5 | The Ideology of Coupledom

Law, policy, and social norms privilege romantic coupledom and the nuclear family as the most important relationships in people's lives and the ones where they are expected to receive most of their care and support. To build a less couple-centric world, we will need to dismantle these institutional hierarchies while building broader social safety nets; it's not enough just to try and accommodate a wider variety of pairings within the couple form, while keeping coupledom as the primary way of deciding who deserves care.

Question: How would you imagine your ideal way of setting up your interpersonal relationships? Would you spend most of your time alone, with one other person, with many people? If that's not how your life is now, what stands in your way?

Action: Looking at the "Relationship Anarchy Smörgåsbord," identify some relationship ingredients you need or want more of in your life. Are there people you already know who you might be able to share those things with, or will you need to seek out new relationships?

6 | Shredded Social Safety Nets

Neoliberalism has dismantled collective institutions that once met people's basic needs. This unravelling of social safety nets makes friendship harder by draining people's time, energy, and material capacity to care for each other. Even worse, it's made its way into our hearts, trying to make us believe we should be able to do everything ourselves and shouldn't rely on each other. Across the world, neoliberal policies have caused communities to fracture, severing bonds of friendship and community. Care must be organized at scale so that we can all get what we need, regardless of how popular or charismatic we are.

Question: Do you have a safety net you could fall back on if things in your life suddenly got a lot harder?

Action: Sometimes, I've been shocked to learn after the fact that a friend was going through a crisis and I hadn't known. Pick one or more friends and promise each other to let each other know when you need help so that you can be there for each other or figure out another way for them to get what they need.

7 | Lonely, Expensive Homes

When housing is cheap, we have more space in our lives to create art, try new things, leave bad relationships, and be better friends. The more expensive our housing is, the more both our lives and our imaginations are constrained. Living with others fosters both deeper and broader connections. While lonely convenience feels compelling, messy interdependence is a much better choice.

Question: Have you ever lived in a more communal housing arrangement? If not, what do you imagine you'd like or find difficult about it?

Action: I don't know if you ever did this, but when I was a kid I loved drawing designs for dream homes, which often featured a lot of slides and secret passages. Design a living space you'd enjoy sharing with people beyond a partner or family, making it as practical or imaginative as you'd like.

8 | Work, the Joy-Eater

Work absorbs time, energy, and attention in ways that crowd out friendships, care, creativity, and everything else that gives life meaning. Because housing costs, debt, and weak social safety nets leave people with little slack, work becomes hard to refuse or deprioritize, even when it contradicts our core values. Reorienting life away from work requires both personal shifts in how we spend our time and a collective shift toward building shared resilience.

Question: Have there been times in your life when paid work was a larger or smaller part of your life than it is now? How were your friendships different in those times than they currently are?

Action: Design a schedule for an ideal week in your life if you only had to do paid work for 10 hours a week. What would you like to do with the rest of your time?

9 | Divesting from Whiteness

Under white supremacy, white people are encouraged to trade interconnectedness and mutual responsibility and care for material gain. Unlearning these lessons involves moving from a concept of safety grounded in self-reliance to one based in interdependence. The Dish With One Spoon framework presents an alternative way of looking at the world based on shared responsibility. Divesting from whiteness involves slowly relearning relational ways of living, accepting discomfort and risk, and building ethical relationships rather than seeking security through isolation.

Question: Whether or not you are white, what values do you connect with whiteness in our white supremacist world? Do you find these showing up in your own life even if they're not the values you personally identify with?

Action: Learn whether the place you live or the place where you grew up is governed by any treaties, and if so, what guidance they give on how to be in good relationship with the land you live on and everyone you share it with.

10 | Investing in Shared Resources

Private ownership and resource hoarding weaken community. Pooling resources through shared spaces, tools, and projects is ultimately more sustainable, more practical, and more fun, although it also involves inconvenience and frustration.

Question: What do you wish you could access without having to buy or own it yourself? A trampoline, an expensive tool, a musical instrument, a cabin by a lake, an assistive device?

Action: Identify a specialized skill you have, a resource you have in abundance, or a special tool you own and could lend out and make a plan for how you can make it available to others.

11 | Organizing Together

Affinity groups and collectives create spaces where friendship and organizing overlap, offering accountability, collective decision making, and practical support for mutual goals. Combining friendship (and food!) with organizing can accomplish what Toni Cade Bambara calls "making the revolution irresistible."

Question: When have you felt most welcome, or most enjoyed yourself, in an organizing/activism/movement space? What made it feel good?

Action: The next time you go to a protest or organizing meeting, bring food to share.

12 | Planning Together

Contrary to the stereotype of the solitary prepper, community preparedness is a shared practice of care and trust. Practising preparedness together through small, low-stakes steps builds skills and habits that will help us weather more serious crises together. We need to relinquish our desire for convenience and embrace messy, inconvenient, vulnerable interdependence.

Question: What do you need, whether material things, plans, or relationships, to be better able to withstand a disaster?

Action: One of the people in this chapter began her community preparedness project by researching what the most likely types of disaster were in her area, and what her city's emergency plans for them were. Try finding this out for where you live.

13 | Learning How (and Why) to Repair

Friendship is hard to sustain when we don't know how, or even why, to repair breaches in relationship. Repair requires patience, curiosity, and the willingness to tolerate discomfort and difficult emotions like shame. Learning to sustain bonds across difference involves practising honesty and compassion in lower-stakes moments, expanding the emotional capacity to hold both our mistakes and our loved ones' imperfections at once.

Question: When is it important to you to mend relationships when they fall into disrepair, and when are you content to burn bridges?

Action: Thinking of a relationship in your life that fell apart, what do you think would have needed to happen differently for it to have been restored instead?

14 | Building Community and Friendship across Difference

Community and friendship are often confused for one another, but community requires us to figure out how to share space with people who are different from us and who we may not even like. This requires patience, willingness to repair, and an ability to endure discomfort. Religious spaces can provide a container for these types of bonds to form and grow, but they're not the only places this can happen.

Question: How can secular spaces do the same work of building bonds of community as religious spaces?

Action: If you've never been part of a religious, cultural, or other group that gave you a sense of tight-knit community and mutual care, find someone in your life who has and talk to them about what it's like.

15 | Returning to Ritual, Celebration, and Grief

Ritual and collective ceremony provide a container for sharing deeper experiences of collective joy, grief, and care. They give us opportunities to co-regulate, mark milestones, and build continuity across time.

Question: Have you experienced a ritual or celebration that has helped you understand, process, and find meaning in an event or aspect of your life?

Action: Think of something that is coming up, whether it's a time of year like solstice or equinox, the anniversary of something joyful or difficult, or a life change like graduating, moving, or finalizing a divorce. Work with a friend to design a ritual that could mark the event, and invite people who you'd like to observe, honour, or celebrate it with.

16 | Imagining a New World as This One Crumbles

Moments of collective action give us tantalizing glimpses of alternative ways of being, which we are also building in those moments. Facing accelerating environmental and social crises requires reorienting toward interdependence, cultivating networks of care and reciprocity. When we build broader, deeper, more varied connections, we begin creating the worlds we hope to inhabit. While we are all acted upon by powerful forces of structural injustice, we still have infinite opportunities to choose interconnectedness over isolation.

Question: When Ursula K. Le Guin was asked what she would change about any of her books, she told the interviewer that in her anarchist utopian sci-fi novel *The Dispossessed*, she envisioned, but couldn't find a way to work into the text, that the book's setting included "communal pickle barrels at street corners in the big towns, restocked by whoever in the community has made or kept more pickles than they need." Leaving aside the bigger questions of what kind of world you'd like to live in, what is one small, concrete detail you envision about that world?

Action: Gotcha! Now go out and make that small detail happen. Start building those pickle barrels!

Further Reading

Nonfiction

Adereth, Maya. "The United States Has a Long History of Mutual Aid Organizing." *Jacobin Magazine*, June 14, 2020. jacobin.com/2020/06/mutual-aid-united-states-unions.

Ahenakew, Cash, Elwood Jimmy, Vanessa Andreotti, and Sharon Stein. *Towards Scarring Our Collective Soul Wound*. Musagetes, 2019.

American Friends Service Committee. "Climate Displacement Advocacy Memo." November 9, 2022. refugeerights.org/wp-content/uploads/2022/11/Climate-Displacement-Advocacy-Memo-Nov-2022.pdf.

Bell, Sierra. *The Plight of Climate Refugees: A Moral Call to Action*. University of New Mexico Digital Repository. digitalrepository.unm.edu/cgi/viewcontent.cgi?article=1033&context=shri_publications.

Berlant, Lauren. "Do You Intend to Die? Lauren Berlant on Intimacy after Suicide." *King's Review*, March 4, 2015. kingsreview.co.uk/essays/do-you-intend-to-die-lauren-berlant-on-intimacy-after-suicide.

Bernstein Sycamore, Mattilda. *The Freezer Door*. Semiotext(e), 2020.

Brain, Robert. *Friends and Lovers*. Paladin, 1977.

Brown, Sherronda J. *Refusing Compulsory Sexuality: A Black Asexual Lens on Our Sex-Obsessed Culture*. North Atlantic Books, 2022.

Chatzidakis, Andreas, Jamie Hakim, Jo Littler, Catherine Rottenberg, and Lynne Segal. *The Care Manifesto: The Politics of Interdependence*. Verso, 2020.

Chasin, C.J. "Ace-Aro Friendly Society: Sexual Orientation and Identity Politics." *Asexualities: Feminist and Queer Perspectives, Revised and Expanded Ten-Year Anniversary Edition*. Routledge, 2024. chasin.ca/cj/Chasin_Ace-Aro-Friendly_Society_Sexual-Orientation_2024.pdf.

Chen, Ching-In, Jai Dulani, and Leah Lakshmi Piepzna-Samarasinha, eds. *The Revolution Starts at Home: Confronting Intimate Violence Within Activist Communities*. South End Press, 2011.

Cohen Booth, Rachel. "How Volunteerism and Charity Donations Are Failing to Drive Systemic Change." *Vox Culture*, August 26, 2024. vox.com/culture/368201/volunteer-charity-donations-systemic-change-activism-nonprofits-loneliness-philanthropy.

Cohen, Rhaina. *The Other Significant Others: Reimagining Life with Friendship at the Center*. St. Martin's Press, 2024.

Crabb, Cindy. *The Encyclopedia of Doris*. Doris Press, 2011.

Davis, Mike. *Planet of Slums*. Verso, 2006.

Dean, Jodi. "Gay Love Conquers All." *The Contemporary Condition*, 2013. contemporarycondition.blogspot.com/2013/07/gay-love-conquers-all.html.

Delany, Samuel R. *Times Square Red, Times Square Blue*. New York University Press, 2019.

Dixon, Ejeris, and Leah Lakshmi Piepzna-Samarasinha, eds. *Beyond Survival: Strategies and Stories from the Transformative Justice Movement*. AK Press, 2020.

"Domestic Workers Bill of Rights." *Domestic Workers Alliance*. domesticworkers.org/programs-and-campaigns/developing-policy-solutions/domestic-workers-bill-of-rights/.

Ghaadbian, Weyam, and Jovida Ross. *Turning Towards Each Other: A Conflict Workbook*. AK Press, 2022.

Greenfield, Adam. *Lifehouse: Taking Care of Ourselves in a World on Fire*. Verso, 2024.

Hassan, Shira. *Saving Our Own Lives: A Liberatory Practice of Harm Reduction*. Haymarket Books, 2022.

Heim Shepard, Benjamin. *On Activism, Friendships, and Fighting: Oral Histories, Strategies, And Conflicts*. Common Notions, 2025.

Jaffe, Sarah. *Work Won't Love You Back: How Devotion to Our Jobs Keeps Us Exploited, Exhausted, and Alone*. Bold Type Books, 2022.

Kaba, Mariame, and Shira Hassan. *Fumbling Towards Repair: A Workbook for Community Accountability Facilitators*. Project NIA, Just Practice, 2019.

Kahan, Benjamin. *Celibacies: American Modernism and Sexual Life*. Duke University Press, 2014.

Klinenberg, Eric. *Palaces for the People: How Social Infrastructure Can Help Fight Inequality, Polarization, and the Decline of Civic Life*. Crown Publishing Group, 2018.

Kropotkin, Peter. *Mutual Aid: A Factor of Evolution.* Penguin Group, 2024.

Liming, Sheila. *Hanging out: The Radical Power of Killing Time.* Melville House Publishing, 2024.

Livni, Ephrat. "We're Treating Friendships Like Transactions, and It's Ruining Relationships." *Quartz*, July 20, 2022. qz.com/1352437/our-friends-arent-toxic-theyre-just-human.

Loreto, Nora. "Navigating Conflict in Activist Spaces." *Nora Loreto Substack*, May 22, 2025. noraloreto.substack.com/p/navigating-conflict-in-activist-spaces.

Milstein, Cindy Barukh. *Constellations of Care: Anarcha-Feminism in Practice.* Pluto Press, 2024.

___. *There Is Nothing So Whole as a Broken Heart: Mending the World as Jewish Anarchists.* AK Press, 2021.

O'Brien, M.E. *Family Abolition: Capitalism and the Communizing of Care.* Pluto Press, 2022.

Orlando, Lisa. "The Asexual Manifesto," 1972. asexualagenda.wordpress.com/2019/08/01/lisa-orlando-author-of-the-asexual-manifesto-1972/

Osberg, Molly. "These Nine People Gave Up the Middle-Class Dream. Was It Worth It?" *Talking Points Memo*, 2025. talkingpointsmemo.com/theslice/these-nine-people-gave-up-middle-class-dream-for-collective-living-was-it-worth-it.

Oshun Muyiwa, Deidra. "Many Hands Make Little Work: Exploring Mutual Aid and Mutual Assistance and Its Connection to Black Mother Activism." *Can You Make It From Scratch?*, June 9, 2017. canyoumakeitfromscratch.blog/2017/06/09/many-hands-make-little-work-exploring-mutual-aid-and-mutual-assistance-and-its-connection-to-black-mother-activism/.

Persinette. "Less TikTok, More Screaming." *Persinette Substack*. March 8, 2023. persinette.substack.com/p/less-tiktok-more-screaming.

Putnam, Robert D. *Bowling Alone: The Collapse and Revival of American Community.* Simon & Schuster, 2000.

Schulman, Sarah. *Conflict Is Not Abuse: Overstating Harm, Community Responsibility, and the Duty of Repair.* Arsenal Pulp Press, 2016.

___. *The Gentrification of the Mind: Witness to a Lost Imagination.* University of California Press, 2012.

Segal, Erin, Chris Hoff, and Julie Cho, eds. *An Encyclopedia of Radical Helping*. Thick Press, 2024.
Spade, Dean. *Love in a F*cked-Up World: How to Build Relationships, Hook Up, and Raise Hell Together*. Algonquin Books, 2024.
___. *Mutual Aid: Building Solidarity During This Crisis (and the Next)*. Verso, 2020.

Fiction

Capewell, Ocean. *The Most Beautiful Rot*. Self-published, 2014.
Corele, Lyn, and Jimmy Cooper, eds. *Make the Golf Course a Public Sex Forest!* Self-published, 2023.
Gloss, Molly. *The Dazzle of Day*. Saga Press, 2019.
Kern, Sim. *The Free People's Village*. Levine Querido, 2023.
Schulman, Sarah. *Rat Bohemia*. Arsenal Pulp Press, 2021.

Zines

Cometbus, Aaron. *Post-Mortem (Cometbus #59)*. Self-published, 2020.
et Nihil, Omnes. *Extensive Notes on Some Aspects of... Neoliberalism, Homonormativity & Ace Discourse Zine*. Self-published, 2016.
galaxy, nebula. *Nebula Thoughts*. Self-published, 2023.
Gray, Twoey, Rea Sweets, and Jaden Tsan, eds. *PRUDEmag Issue #1*. Self-published, 2019.
___. *PRUDEmag Issue #2*. Self-published, 2023.
Mixed Rice Zines. *Queering Friendships #3*. Self-published, 2024.

Podcasts

It Did Happen Here
Live Like the World Is Dying
Movement Memos

Notes

Preface

1 Tori Latham, "The Scheduling Woes of Adult Friendship," *The Atlantic*, July 23, 2019, theatlantic.com/family/archive/2019/07/planning-friend-hangouts-google-calendar/594586/Catherine Pearson, "How to Make, and Keep, Friends in Adulthood," *New York Times*, October 1, 2022, nytimes.com/2022/10/01/well/live/how-to-make-friends-adult.html; Daisy Jones, "Why Does Growing Up and Settling Down Mean Losing a Certain Closeness with Your Friends?" *Vogue*, March 27, 2023, vogue.com/article/growing-up-settling-down-losing-closeness-with-friends.

Chapter 1

1 Henning Bech, *When Men Meet: Homosexuality and Modernity* (University of Chicago Press, 1997), quoted in Peter Nardi, *Gay Men's Friendships: Invincible Communities* (University of Chicago Press, 1999), 65.
2 Angela Chen, *Ace: What Asexuality Reveals about Desire, Society, and the Meaning of Sex* (Beacon Press, 2020, epub), chap. 7, "Romance, Reconsidered."
3 Marina Doucerain, Andrew Ryder, and Catherine Amiot, "What Are Friends for in Russia Versus Canada?: An Approach for Documenting Cross-Cultural Differences," *Cross-Cultural Research* 55, 6 (June 2021) DOI: 10.1177/10693971211024599.
4 Glen Adams and Victoria C. Plaut, "The Cultural Grounding of Personal Relationship: Friendship in North American and West African Worlds," *Personal Relationships* 10, 3 (2003), 3. DOI: 10.1111/1475-6811.00053.

Chapter 2

1 Gayle Rubin, "The Catacombs: A Temple of the Butthole," in *Leatherfolk: Radical Sex, People, Politics, and Practice*, ed. Mark Thompson (Alyson Publications, 1991), 139.
2 O'Mara, Aley. *Asexual Manifesto 2022: Radical Asexual Politics, 50 Years On*. (Art Over Chaos Publishing, 2023).
3 Omnes et Nihil defines queerplatonic relationships as "non-normative relationships that are not romantic relationships and also not properly or adequately expressed by 'friendship' either. People of any sexual or romantic orientation can do QP relationships, and the relationships may or may not involve anything sexual" (*Queerplatonic Zucchinis: A Short Primer*, self-published, 2014).
4 Chen, *Ace*, chap. 7.
5 C.S. Lewis, *The Four Loves* (Geoffrey Bles, 1960), 7.
6 For example, "One of the most distinctive features of the current regime under which we live is the prominence of heterosexuality and homosexuality as central, organizing categories of thought, behavior, and erotic subjectivity. The rise to dominance of those categories represents a relatively recent and culturally specific development, yet it has left little trace in our consciousness of its novelty. As a result, not only do we have a hard time understanding the logic at work in other historical cultures' organizations of sex and gender, but we have an even harder time understanding our own inability to understand them" (David M. Halperin, *How to Do the History of Homosexuality* [University of Chicago Press, 2002], 3. For context on his "we," Halperin is a white gay American man.
7 Lilian Faderman's *Surpassing the Love of Men: Romantic Friendship and Love Between Women from the Renaissance to the Present* looks at this question in detail. In the book's introduction, she writes, "My studies also led me to conclude that it is in our century that love has come to be perceived as a refinement of the sexual impulse, but in many other centuries romantic love and sexual impulse were often considered unrelated. Certainly, the degree of sexual expression among romantic friends must have varied, just as it does among women who are avowedly lesbian today. However, it is likely that most love relationships between women during previous eras, when females were encouraged to force any

sexual drive they might have to remain latent, were less physical than they are in our times. But the lack of overt sexual expression in these romantic friendships could not discount the seriousness or the intensity of the women's passions toward each other — or the fact that if by 'lesbian' we mean an all-consuming emotional relationship in which two women are devoted to each other above anyone else, these ubiquitous sixteenth-, seventeenth-, eighteenth-, and nineteenth-century romantic friendships were 'lesbian'" Morrow, 1981, 19).

8 Wesley Hill, *Spiritual Friendship: Finding Love in the Church as a Celibate Gay Christian* (Baker Books, 2015), xix.

Chapter 3

1 Edmund White, *States of Desire: Travels in Gay America* (Dutton, 1980), 263.
2 Lauren Berger, Lisa Hohmann, and Wyndol Furman, "Friendship," *Britannica*, britannica.com/topic/friendship.
3 Lewis, *The Four Loves*, 72.

Chapter 4

1 Edmund White, *The Beautiful Room Is Empty* (Quality Paperback Book Club, 1993), 105.
2 Nardi, *Gay Mens' Friendships*, 3.
3 Kath Weston, *Families We Choose: Lesbians, Gays, Kinship* (Columbia University Press, 1991), xiv.
4 Weston, *Families We Choose*, 113.
5 "Chosen Family," Google Books Ngram Viewer, books.google.com/ngrams/graph?content=%22chosen+family%22&year_start=1800&year_end=2022&corpus=en&smoothing=3.
6 For example, "the Lord's chosen family will not be beguiled from their steadfastness" (Charles Haddon Spurgeon, *The Saint and His Saviour: The Progress of the Soul in the Knowledge of Jesus* [Sheldon, Blakeman, 1857], 242.
7 "Revolutionary Activities Directed Toward the Administration of Penal or Correctional Systems: Hearings, Ninety-third Congress, First Session," US Government Printing Office, 1973, hdl.handle.net/2027/umn.31951d03673128e.

8 The Sentencing Project, *Mass Incarceration Trends*, May 21, 2024, sentencingproject.org/reports/mass-incarceration-trends/.
9 "Revolutionary Activities," 1318.
10 Cari Shane, "The First Self-Proclaimed Drag Queen Was a Formerly Enslaved Man," *Smithsonian Magazine*, smithsonianmag.com/history/the-first-self-proclaimed-drag-queen-was-a-formerly-enslaved-man-180982311/.
11 Ricky Tucker, *And the Category Is...: Inside New York's Vogue, House, and Ballroom Community* (Beacon Press, 2022), 89–90.
12 bell hooks, *Black Looks: Race and Representation* (South End Press, 1992), 152.
13 Weston, *Families We Choose*, 108.
14 Weston, *Families We Choose*, 113.
15 Michel Foucault, "Sexual Choice, Sexual Act: An Interview with Michel Foucault," interview by James O'Higgins, *Salmagundi* 58/59 (Fall 1982–Winter 1983), salmagundi.skidmore.edu/articles/11-sexual-choice-sexual-act.
16 Weston, *Families We Choose*, 111.
17 Juan Carlos Pérez Cortés, *Relationship Anarchy: Occupy Intimacy!*, self-published, 2022, chap. 1.2 and 5.2, theanarchistlibrary.org/library/juan-carlo-perez-cortez-relationship-anarchy.
18 Nardi, *Gay Men's Friendships*, 47.

Chapter 5

1 Ameya Nagarajan, "If We Privileged Friendship," in Shilpa Phadke and Nithila Kanagasabai, eds., *Yaari: An Anthology on Friendship by Women and Queer Folx* (Yoda Press, 2023), 31.
2 BlackDeer, Autumn, LinkedIn, October 21, 2024, linkedin.com/posts/drblackdeer_in-a-capitalist-society-your-connections-activity-7254216177973919745-cF-I/.
3 Christopher Bollen, "Ask a Sane Person: Naomi Klein Is Not Ready to Give Up the Fight," *Interview Magazine*, May 8, 2020, interviewmagazine.com/culture/ask-a-sane-person-naomi-klein-is-not-ready-to-give-up-the-fight.
4 Elizabeth Brake, *Minimizing Marriage: Marriage, Morality, and the Law* (Oxford University Press, 2012),158.

5 Brake, *Minimizing Marriage*, 89; *Quirkyalone: A Manifesto for Uncompromising Romantics* is a 2004 book by Sasha Cagen, about and for the "person who enjoys being single (but is not opposed to being in a relationship) and generally prefers to be alone rather than date for the sake of being in a couple" (HarperOne, 2004); *Urban Tribes: A Generation Redefines Friendship, Family, and Commitment* by Ethan Watters is a 2003 book about "the cultural and social forces that have kept the current generation away from the altar and offering an intriguing portrait of so-called "Urban Tribes," closely knit communities of friends that evolve during the period between college and marriage" (Bloomsbury, 2003).

6 Brake, *Minimizing Marriage*, 5.

7 Brake, *Minimizing Marriage*, 7.

8 K.V. Rao and Alfred Demaris, "Coital Frequency among Married and Cohabiting Couples in the United States," *Journal of Biosocial Science* 2, 27, 1995, DOI: 10.1017/s0021932000022653

9 "Is Gay Marriage Racist? A Conversation with Marlon M. Bailey, Priya Kandaswamy, and Mattie Udora Richardson," in Mattilda Bernstein Sycamore, ed., *That's Revolting!: Queer Strategies for Resisting Assimilation* (Soft Skull Press, 2004), 115–116.

10 Community Legal Education Ontario, "Social Assistance Rules about Couples," February 2025, cleo.on.ca/en/publications/cohab-en/all.

11 Yasmin Nair, "Your Sex Is Not Radical," *YasminNair.com*, June 28, 2015, yasminnair.com/your-sex-is-not-radical/. Nair is a member of Against Equality, a collective "focused on critiquing mainstream gay and lesbian politics…. dislodging the centrality of equality rhetoric and challenging the demand for inclusion in the institution of marriage, the US military, and the prison industrial complex," who were influential in shaping the way I think about queer relationships in a straight world.

12 Hannah Black, "The Loves of Others," *The New Inquiry*, June 22, 2018, thenewinquiry.com/the-loves-of-others/.

13 Dean Spade, "For Lovers and Fighters," in Melody Berger, ed., *We Don't Need Another Wave: Dispatches from the Next Generation of Feminists* (Seal Press, 2010), 31.

14 The Relationship Anarchy Smörgåsbord was originated by Lyrica Lawrence and Heather Orr of Vancouver Polyamory in December

2016. Subsequent versions have been updated by Maxx Hill, "with the guidance of many, including the Relationship Anarchy, Polyamory and Solo Polyamory Facebook Groups." In this book, I refer to version 6. We couldn't reprint the image in this book due to formatting constraints, but you can find the Smörgåsbord in a variety of languages and formats at tinyurl.com/rasmorgasbord.

Chapter 6

1 Sarah Schulman, *The Fantasy and Necessity of Solidarity* (Penguin Random House, 2025, epub) Ch. 1, "Solidarity: Fantasy and Necessity."

2 Margaret Thatcher, interview by Douglas Keay, *Woman's Own*, September 23, 1987, margaretthatcher.org/document%2F106689.

3 Gary Gerstle, *The Rise and Fall of the Neoliberal Order: America and the World in the Free Market Era* (Oxford University Press, 2022), 5.

4 Bruce Rogers-Vaughn, *Caring for Souls in a Neoliberal Age* (Palgrave Macmillan, 2016), 6.

5 Rogers-Vaughn, *Caring for Souls in a Neoliberal Age*, 1.

6 Rogers-Vaughn, *Caring for Souls in a Neoliberal Age*, 3.

7 Rogers-Vaughn, *Caring for Souls in a Neoliberal Age*, 17.

8 Wendy Brown, *Undoing the Demos: Neoliberalism's Stealth Revolution* (Zone Books, 2015), 37.

9 Nora Loreto., *The Social Safety Net: Canada in Decline Book One* (Dundurn Press, 2024, epub), "Introduction," .

10 Rana Foroohar. , "Globalization's True Believers Are Having Second Thoughts," *Time*, June 3, 2016. , https://time.com/4356816/neoliberalism-imf-globalization/.

11 Jonathan D. Ostry, Prakash Loungani, and Davide Furceri, "Neoliberalism: Oversold?" *Finance & Development*, 53, 2 (June 2016), imf.org/external/pubs/ft/fandd/2016/06/ostry.htm.

12 *Not All Gaps Are Created Equal: The True Value of Care Work,* Oxfam International, 2022, oxfam.org/en/not-all-gaps-are-created-equal-true-value-care-work.

13 United Nations High Commissioner for Refugees, *Climate Change and Displacement,* unhcr.org/what-we-do/build-better-futures/climate-change-and-displacement.

14 Leah Lakshmi Piepzna-Samarasinha. *Care Work: Dreaming Disability Justice*. (Arsenal Pulp Press, 2018), 42, 45.
15 Piepzna-Samarasinha, *Care Work*, 46
16 Loreto, *The Social Safety Net*, ch. 1, "From Before Confederation to 1945."
17 Eric Seiferth, "The Centuries-Old Origins of New Orleans Second Lines," *The Historic New Orleans Collection*, February 24, 2021, hnoc.org/publishing/first-draft/where-do-second-lines-come-origins-go-back-more-200-years.
18 Charles M. Tatum, *Chicano Popular Culture: Que Hable el Pueblo* (University of Arizona Press, 2001), xix.
19 Meridian Films, "Local 598," *Square Dance History Project*, 1959, squaredancehistory.org/items/show/2089.
20 Kavod v'Nichum, "Chevra Kadisha," kavodvnichum.org/chevra-kadisha/.

Chapter 7

1 Sky Fusco, "Against Solitude," *Lord Cowboy Substack*, November 22, 2023. lordcowboy.substack.com/p/against-solitude.
2 Samuel R. Delany, *The Motion of Light in Water: Sex and Science Fiction Writing in the East Village* (University of Minnesota Press, 2004).
3 Delany, *The Motion of Light in Water*, 19.
4 Delany, *The Motion of Light in Water*, 165.
5 Department of Labor, "History of the Minimum Wage in New York State," dol.ny.gov/history-minimum-wage-new-york-state.
6 Diane di Prima, *Recollections of My Life as a Woman: The New York Years* (Penguin Books, 2001), 127.
7 Brennan Leffler and Marianne Dimain, "How Poverty, Not Pain, Is Driving Canadians with Disabilities to Consider Medically-Assisted Death," *Global News*, October 8, 2022, globalnews.ca/news/9176485/poverty-canadians-disabilities-medically-assisted-death/
8 Howard Husock, "What Is a Family? Ask a Zoning Official," American Enterprise Institute, October 26, 2022, aei.org/op-eds/what-is-a-family-ask-a-zoning-official/.
9 Daniel Oleksiuk, *It's (Past) Time for British Columbia to Legalize Roommates*, Sightline Institute, April 15, 2024, sightline.org/2024/04/15/its-past-time-for-british-columbia-to-legalize-roommates/.

10 Canadian Centre for Housing Rights, *Occupancy Rules: Guests, Roommates, Subtenants and Lease Assignments – Ontario Housing Law Basics*, housingrightscanada.com/resources/occupancy-rules-guests-roommates-subtenants-and-lease-assignments-ontario-housing-law-basics/.
11 Michael Waters, "Where Living with Friends Is Still Technically Illegal," *The Atlantic*, May 22, 2023, theatlantic.com/family/archive/2023/05/zoning-laws-nuclear-modern-family-definition/674117/.
12 Waters, "Where Living with Friends Is Still Technically Illegal."
13 Lisa Sibbett, "The Radical Politics of Auntiehood," *The Auntie Bulletin*, September 17, 2024, theauntie.substack.com/p/the-radical-politics-of-auntiehood.

Chapter 8

1 Cindy Crabb, *Doris: An Anthology 1991–2001* (Microcosm Publishing, 2009), 241.
2 Dean Spade, "It's So Queer to Give Away Money," *Tikkun* 25, 4 (July/August2010), 63. deanspade.net/wp-content/uploads/2017/06/Its-So-Queer-to-Give-Away-Money-Tikkun-Magazine.pdf.
3 Eman Abdelhadi and M.E. O'Brien, *Everything for Everyone: An Oral History of the New York Commune, 2052–2072* (Common Notions, 2022).
4 David Graeber and David Wengrow, *The Dawn of Everything: A New History of Humanity.* (Farrar, Straus, and Giroux, 2021); David Graeber, *The Utopia of Rules : On Technology, Stupidity, and the Secret Joys of Bureaucracy* (Melville House, 2015), 89.
5 I was unable to find the source for this, unfortunately!
6 A.J. Ravenelle and K.C. Kowalski, "'It's Not Like Chasing Chanel': Spending Time, Investing in the Self, and Pandemic Epiphanies," *Work and Occupations 50, 2* (September 15, 2022), doi.org/10.1177/07308884221125246; Samantha Masunaga and Sean Greene, "Quiet Quitting. RTO. Coffee Badging. What This New Vocabulary Says about Your Workplace," *Los Angeles Times*, March 4, 2024, latimes.com/business/story/2024-03-04/quiet-quitting-rto-coffee-badging-what-this-new-vocabulary-says-about-the-workplace.

7 Amelia Horgan, *Lost in Work: Escaping Capitalism* (Pluto Press,2021, epub), ch. 4, "What Does Work Do to Us as Individuals?"

Part Three

1 Phadke and Kanagasabai, Yaari, 29.
2 Kurt Vonnegut, *God Bless You, Dr. Kevorkian* (Seven Stories Press, 1999), 15.
3 CrimethInc., "How to Form an Affinity Group: The Essential Building Block of Anarchist Organization," February 6, 2017, crimethinc.com/2017/02/06/how-to-form-an-affinity-group-the-essential-building-block-of-anarchist-organization.

Chapter 9

1 James Baldwin, "Letter from a Region in My Mind." *New Yorker*, November 9, 1962, newyorker.com/magazine/1962/11/17/letter-from-a-region-in-my-mind.
2 Stefano Harney and Fred Moten, *The Undercommons: Fugitive Planning & Black Study* (Autonomedia/Minor Compositions, 2013), 140–41.
3 Fred Glover, "A Dish with One Spoon," *The Canadian Encyclopedia,* March 31, 2020, thecanadianencyclopedia.ca/en/article/a-dish-with-one-spoon.
4 Patty Krawec, *Becoming Kin: An Indigenous Call to Unforgetting the Past and Reimagining Our Future* (Broadleaf Books, 2022), 147.
5 "Patty Krawec," transatlanticagency.com/clients/speakers/patty-krawec/.

Chapter 10

1 Jeremy Williams, "Every Child on Their Own Trampoline," *The Earthbound Report*, April 8, 2021, earthbound.report/2021/04/08/every-child-on-their-own-trampoline/.
2 Williams, "Every child on their own trampoline."
3 Mike Davis, "Who Will Build the Ark?" *New Left Review* 61 (Jan/Feb 2010), newleftreview.org/issues/ii61/articles/mike-davis-who-will-build-the-ark.
4 Simon Octeau and Lena Payen, "Les programmes locaux d'implantation de ruelles vertes a Montreal," 2018, 13,

ruellesvertesdemontreal.ca/_files/ugd/87ef24_22da398a955741118924c4abe30a7979.pdf.

5 Simon Octeau and Lena Payen, "Guide d'aménagement de ruelles vertes et actives," 2018, 16, ruellesvertesdemontreal.ca/_files/ugd/87ef24_0cefcb4bda1c4215ace9f133c0527dbe.pdf.

6 Workshop for Independent Publishing, wipmpls.com/.

7 India Johnson, *Own the Means of Production and Share It: Why & How Artists Should Pool Resources* (Late Night Copies Press, 2023).

8 Dick's Lending Library, "About," dickslendinglibrary.com/about/.

Chapter 11

1 Aurora Levins Morales, "V'ahavta," July 25, 2016, auroralevinsmorales.com/blog/vahavta.

2 Cindy Barukh Milstein, ed., *Don't Just Do Nothing: 20 Things You Can Do to Counter Fascism — Yes, You! Yes, Now*, self-published, 2024.

3 Garrett Bucks, "Soup and Pie and Nobody Left Behind," *The White Pages Substack*, November 26, 2024, thewhitepages.net/p/soup-and-pie-and-nobody-left-behind.

4 Toni Cade Bambara and Thabiti Lewis, "An Interview with Toni Cade Bambara: Kay Bonetti," *Conversations with Toni Cade Bambara* (University Press of Mississippi, 2012), 35.

5 Mariame Kaba, "Some Actions That Are Not Protesting or Voting," docs.google.com/document/u/0/d/1OSWxykA1WHOi0vTPLAJDaCeVhR3uSfh7PhlCj4t4yT0/mobilebasic.

6 CrimethInc, "How to Form an Affinity Group."

7 Murray Bookchin, *The Spanish Anarchists: The Heroic Years 1868–1936* (Harper & Row, 1978), 116–17.

8 Eve Hinderer, "Ben Morea, Black Mask and Motherfucker: A Saga of the '60s Lower East Side," *16 Beaver*, June 7, 2004, web.archive.org/web/20090425191200/http://www.16beavergroup.org/monday/archives/001031print.html.

9 CrimethInc., "How to Form an Affinity Group."

10 Kipton Jensen and Preston King, "Beloved Community: Martin Luther King, Howard Thurman, and Josiah Royce," *AMITY: The Journal of Friendship Studies*, 4, 1, 15–31, doi:10.5518/AMITY/20.

11 Southerners on New Ground, "Alchemy: The Elements of Creating

Collective Space," 2019, southernersonnewground.org/wp-content/uploads/2019/07/SONG-Alchemy-The-Elements-of-Creating-Collective-Space.pdf.

12 Lewis, *The Four Loves*, 94.

Chapter 12

1 Kelly Hayes and Mariame Kaba, *Let This Radicalize You: Organizing and the Revolution of Reciprocal Care* (Haymarket Books, 2023), 33.

2 Transition US and New Stories, *Ready Together: An Emergency Preparedness Handbook for You and Your Neighbors*, November 2020, mutualaiddisasterrelief.org/wp-content/uploads/2021/10/Ready-Together-An-Emergency-Preparedness-Handbook-for-You-and-Your-Neighbors.pdf.

3 I am thinking for example about Sarah Schulman's *Rat Bohemia* (Arsenal Pulp, 1995).

4 Krissi Driver, "A Korean Secret to Keeping Friendships Strong: Savings Groups," *New York Times*, June 18, 2024, nytimes.com/2024/06/18/business/mutual-funds/saving-korea-gyemoim.html.

5 carly boyce, *helping your friends who sometimes wanna die maybe not die*, self-published, 2019.

6 boyce, *helping your friends who sometimes wanna die maybe not die*, 1.

Chapter 13

1 Bryn Kelly, "Diving into the Wreck," March 30, 2012, brynkelly-blog.tumblr.com/post/20162901452/diving-into-the-wreck.

2 rayne fisher-quann, "no good alone," *internet princess Substack*, April 3, 2023, internetprincess.substack.com/p/no-good-alone.

3 Ayesha Khan, "You Don't Need to 'Fill Your Cup First' to Seek or Be in Community," *Cosmic Anarchy Substack*, December 19, 2024, wokescientist.substack.com/p/you-dont-need-to-fill-your-cup-first.

4 Karen Riddell, "End That Friendship! Some Friendships Are Bad for You," *Psychology Today*, July 14, 2017, psychologytoday.com/us/blog/friendship-observation/201707/end-friendship.

5 James Hardwick, "Canadians Are Living Through a People's Recession: Why Your Bank Account Feels the Squeeze while GDP Rises," *Canadian Dimension*, October 23, 2025, canadiandimension.com/

articles/view/canadians-are-on-year-three-of-a-peoples-recession.
6 Michael Hobbes, "The Epidemic of Gay Loneliness," *HuffPost Highline*, March 2017, highline.huffingtonpost.com/articles/en/gay-loneliness/.
7 UAF Justice, *A Healing Journey for Alaska Natives: Community Responses with Victims & Offenders*, YouTube video, 1:04, April 30, 2013, youtube.com/watch?v=xKKnLCUrYqA.
8 Elise Granata, "Community Is about What We Are Willing to Feel," *Group Hug Substack*, January 16, 2024, grouphug.substack.com/p/community-is-about-what-we-are-willing.
9 Alexis Shotwell, "Claiming Bad Kin: Solidarity from Complicit Locations," *Bearing: The Society for the Diffusion of Useful Knowledge* 3 (March 2019).
10 Krawec, *Becoming Kin*, 19.

Chapter 14

1 Moe Bowstern, "Living in the Backswing," *Subversion Through Friendliness Substack*, January 18, 2025, moebowstern.substack.com/p/living-in-the-backswing.
2 fangmeli, X, April 21, 2019, x.com/pangmeli/status/1119978801851699200.
3 Casey Plett, *On Community* (Biblioasis, 2023, epub), "Needs," 2.
4 Matthew Shaer, "Why Is the Loneliness Epidemic So Hard to Cure?" *New York Times,* August 27, 2024, nytimes.com/2024/08/27/magazine/loneliness-epidemic-cure.html.
5 Weston, *Families We Choose*, 123.
6 Anndee Hochman, *Everyday Acts and Small Subversions: Women Reinventing Family, Community and Home* (Eighth Mountain Press, 1994), 67.

Chapter 15

1 Abraham Joshua Heschel, *Who Is Man* (Stanford University Press, 1965), 117.
2 Hochman, *Everyday Acts & Small Subversions*, 176–79.
3 Hochman, *Everyday Acts & Small Subversions*, 174–75.
4 Hochman, *Everyday Acts & Small Subversions*, 99.

Interlude 3

1 Cindy Barukh Milstein, ed., *Ritual as Resistance: 18 Stories of Defending the Sacred*, self-published, 2025.

Chapter 16

1 Bertold Brecht, trans. and ed. by Tom Kuhn and David Constantine, *The Collected Poems of Bertold Brecht* (Liveright Publishing, 2018), 787.
2 Steven Charleston, *We Survived the End of the World: Lessons from Native America on Apocalypse and Hope* (Broadleaf Books, 2023, epub), "Apocalypse: The Mystery and Miracle of Survival."
3 Jem Bendell, "Deep Adaptation: A Map for Navigating Climate Tragedy," revised 2nd edition, July 27, 2020, lifeworth.com/deepadaptation.pdf.
4 Bill McKibben, "Where Should I Live?" *The Crucial Years Substack*, August 5, 2023, billmckibben.substack.com/p/where-should-i-live.
5 Elise Granata, "Did Your Utopia Already Exist?" *Group Hug Substack*, February 20, 2024, grouphug.substack.com/p/did-your-utopia-already-exist.
6 Jon Henley, "Greece's Solidarity Movement: 'It's a Whole New Model – and It's Working,'" *Guardian*, January 23, 2015, theguardian.com/world/2015/jan/23/greece-solidarity-movement-cooperatives-syriza.
7 Robyn Maynard and Leanne Betasamosake Simpson, *Rehearsals for Living* (Vintage Canada, 2023), 36.
8 Rebecca Solnit, *Hope in the Dark: Untold Histories, Wild Possibilities* (Haymarket Books, 2016), 80–81.
9 Samuel R. Delany, *Times Square Red, Times Square Blue 20th Anniversary Edition* (NYU Press, 2019), 57.
10 Annie Dillard, *The Writing Life* (HarperPerennial, 1999), 32.

Glossary

1 "Twenty Questions with Ursula K. Le Guin," *Times Literary Supplement*, March 6 2017, the-tls.com/regular-features/twenty-questions/twenty-questions-ursula-le-guin

Index